simply incredible

vegetarian and vegan creations

chef mark anthony

Simply Incredible © 2012 by Mark Anthony
All rights reserved.

ISBN-13: 978-0-9828791-5-3
ISBN-10: 0-9828791-5-6

Printed in the United States of America

Layout and Cover Design: Lanette Steiner

To order books, request information or comment contact:
Mark Anthony
Box 20861
Las Vegas, NV 89112
E-mail: spicecreator@yahoo.com

Holmes Printing
solutions LLC

8757 County Road 77
Fredericksburg, Ohio 44627
888.473.6870

FOREWORD

Welcome to the simplicity of the healthiest lifestyle on the planet. Simply Incredible. In this book you will find out how easy it really is to go vegan and go healthy. It's time for us to use the common sense that God gave us and start experiencing the joys of great health through the thousands of flavorful sensations He has waiting for us.

More than just providing you with great recipes, I would like to share with you the concepts and practices that will aid you in developing a fun and enjoyable new approach to healthy eating. Station simplicity is a ground breaking idea that will transform your kitchen into an environment that is not only health practical, but will also making your vegan walk efficient, organized, and so much easier to function.

Far too often we complain about how much work it is to cook vegan meals and I just can't think of how hard it must have been years ago before we had the technology we have today in the production area. It's time to make our culinary experiences easy! In today's world, it is so easy to find great manufactured products of every kind, we just need to be careful of the content. I am also so thankful for the simplicity that God has provided for us. There is little prep work in eating an apple, oatmeal, or a salad. So stick to whole natural foods that are easier to prepare and better for you. It is far easier to cook vegan than it is to cook any other lifestyle.

This book is designed to open your mind to the simplicity of vegan cooking. It is far easier than most people could ever imagine. I will be walking you through a lot of extremely simple ways to provide simple, healthy, and attractive meals. Culinary creativity is an easy element to produce when you connect with your imagination.

I pray that you will take this health message to heart and develop stronger convictions to living a healthier life. Because when we are healthier physically, we are healthier mentally, and we have a better spiritual connection with God. Body, mind, and spirit, they really are... all connected.

Mark Anthony

TABLE OF CONTENTS

HEALTH SIMPLICITY

#1 Go Vegan | 7

#2 Reduce Sugar | 13

#3 Reduce Oils | 21

#4 Reduce Salts | 27

#5 Eliminate Alcohol & Drugs | 33

#6 Reduce or Eliminate Caffeine | 37

#7 Eat Your Biggest Meal for Breakfast | 39

#8 Drink Plenty of Water | 41

#9 Exercise Regularly | 49

#10 Get Plenty of Rest | 53

#11 More Sunlight and Air | 55

#12 Pray Every Day | 59

STATION SIMPLICITY

Oatmeal Station | 67

Salad Station | 69

Beans, Rice & Pasta Station | 73

Spice Station | 75

RECIPES SIMPLICITY

Breakfast Simplicity | 81

Oatmeal Simplicity | 99

Granola Simplicity | 109

Gourmet Bar Simplicity | 117

Pancake and Waffle Simplicity | 123

Beverages & Blending Simplicity | 133

Salad Simplicity | 141

Salad Dressing Simplicity | 151

Soup Simplicity | 159

Crock-pot Simplicity | 173

Sauce Simplicity | 181

Appetizer Simplicity | 197

Dips and Salsa Simplicity | 201

Hummus Simplicity | 207

Bruschetta Simplicity | 213

Grilling Simplicity | 221

Sandwich Simplicity | 233

Burger Simplicity | 241

Side Simplicity | 257

Entree Simplicity | 269

Stuffing Stuff Simplicity | 279

Dessert Simplicity | 293

EXTRA EXTRA

3ABN Cooking Program Recipes | 329

Index | 389

go vegan

The best thing that you can ever do to become healthier is to live a vegan lifestyle. Study after study are confirms this fact. More and more doctors are now realizing that not only is vegan the healthiest lifestyle, it can also reverse damages to your body caused by the animal products that literally kill. Even type-2 diabetes can be reversed; cancers can be eliminated; and heart disease can vanish, when you embrace an all vegan lifestyle.

WHAT IS VEGAN VS. VEGETARIAN?

VEGAN:

Vegan is the easiest guideline to follow. Vegans do not consume any animal products whatsoever. Some will not even consume honey or yeast. Vegan is the fastest growing lifestyle group because of its extreme health benefits.

VEGETARIAN:

Vegetarian is a blanket term used to describe a person who does not consume any meat, poultry, fish, or seafood. This grouping includes vegans and the various sub-categories of vegetarian; however, it generally implies someone who has less dietary restrictions than a vegan.

SEMI-VEGETARIAN:

Semi-vegetarian is a vegetarian who consumes dairy products, eggs, chicken, and fish, but does not consume other animal products.

OVO-LACTO-VEGETARIAN:

Ovo-lacto vegetarians do not consume meat, poultry, fish, and seafood, but do consume eggs and milk. This is the largest group of vegetarians.

OVO-VEGETARIAN:

Ovo-vegetarian is a term used to describe someone who would be a vegan if they did not consume eggs.

LACTO-VEGETARIAN:

Lacto-vegetarian is a term used to describe someone who would be a vegan if they did not consume milk.

Going vegan simply means consuming no animal products whatsoever. Some people are claiming to be 100% vegan while others will claim to be 80% vegan or 90% vegan. Well I have news for you, 90% vegan is not vegan. Vegan means going 100% vegan. As much as you would like to give yourself credit where credit is due, you're still not vegan if you're consuming two chicken meals a week or a cream cheese bagel every other morning.

[The rest of the world lives to eat, *while I eat to live.*]
-Socrates

go vegan

There are significant differences between going vegan and going vegetarian. The biggest differences are not only in the foods being consumed, it is also in the results. Vegans do not eat milk, cheese, or eggs. And there are countless statistical facts from all over the world that show how much better off you are to go vegan rather than vegetarian.

Cornell University put it in simple terms for you to understand. The comparison between vegan and vegetarian, they said, if instead of going vegan you are going vegetarian and still consuming milk and cheese, it's like a smoker that goes from 50 cigarettes a day down to 40 cigarettes a day.

You see, you're not really doing your body much good if you are still consuming the milk and cheese. That's because the milk and cheese products still have the fat, animal protein, and cholesterol. It will still contribute to your excessive weight gain and have a severe impact on your overall health because of the cholesterol that coats your arteries, blood cells and brain cells. Study after study confirms that milk and cheese are actually the most unhealthy products on the planet, especially when it comes to cholesterol and animal fat.

CHOLESTEROL - THE #1 KILLER ON THE PLANET

All animals produce cholesterol and when we consume animal products, we are getting a bombardment of cholesterol. Going on a vegan lifestyle with no animal products whatsoever is hands down the best thing you could ever do to get healthy. It's really easy too! Just quit eating animal products and start eating fruits and vegetables. You will soon be eliminating all that life killing element called cholesterol.

Cholesterol is the largest killer on the planet today. 90% of the death rate in America is from killer diseases like cancer, heart diseases, diabetes, and stroke. And the majority of these deaths are directly related to cholesterol. Now the easiest way to lower your cholesterol is to lower your consumption of the animal products that are giving you the cholesterol in the first place! I would recommend a total abstinence from all animal products. If you eliminate all the milk, cheese, eggs, chicken, steak etc. You will live a longer and much healthier life. GUARANTEED! The bottom line, CHOLESTEROL KILLS PEOPLE. So we need to get as far away from it as possible.

I mean let's get real here for a minute! We all know that cholesterol is bad for us and yet we continue to consume it in record amounts. In fact the health of this country and the health of this planet are spiraling down at the exact same rate as our cholesterol increases. It doesn't take a rocket scientist to see the direct comparison between the two.

Cholesterol kills more people than cigarettes every year. Maybe the attorney general should put a warning label on anything with cholesterol in it, like they do for cigarettes; 'Cholesterol Causes Heart Disease' or 'Cholesterol Causes Cancer', or even 'Milk Causes Osteoporosis'. Then maybe people would get the message as to how bad these animal products really are for us.

DR. OZ AGREES

Dr. Oz put it real easy to understand, he said that everyone of us gets cancer cells every day. And when we have the right amount of oxygen in our blood, it removes these cancer cells on a regular basis so they do not become a growth. But when we coat every one of our blood cells and brain cells with this animal fat and cholesterol, then our blood does not get the oxygen it needs and cannot remove the cancer cells. And then boom, we have a cancer growth and killer disease.

It's no wonder, as our cholesterol levels rise as a nation, so does our sickness and killer diseases within our society. Our bodies just can't do the job that they're supposed to be doing. So if you want to live a healthier and more vibrant life, getting off the cholesterol is hands down, the absolute, very best thing that you can ever do.

Many doctors call cancer a vegetable deficiency. Dr. Oz was saying that it is as much a cholesterol overload as it is a vegetable deficiency.

> One-quarter of what you eat keeps you alive.
>
> The other three-quarters
>
> *keeps your doctor alive*
>
> -Ancient Egyptian Proverb

Cholesterol really is the #1 problem on the planet today. So remove all the animal products out of your diet and you will be removing the #1 problem with your diet. Your food will start tasting so much better, because you won't have all that cholesterol surrounding your taste buds.

Do everything you can to get off this cholesterol. I would certainly recommend going on a full blown vegan lifestyle. It works for me, and I have never felt better. My cholesterol went from 263 down to 118 and I have lost almost 80 pounds. Going vegan, with no animal products whatsoever is a lot easier than you think. Stick to the whole foods, stick to the fresh fruits and vegetables. You will actually spend less time in the kitchen, because everything is so much easier to prepare. It's not very hard to cut up a salad, or make a bowl of oatmeal, saute some vegetables instead of a steak. And in today's world, we have hundreds of options when it comes to healthy choices.

Not only does the animal fat and cholesterol surround every one of our blood cells, it surrounds every one of our brain cells.. When we eliminate animal products from our diet, we also remove the hazy coating surrounding our brain cells and that helps us become better thinkers. Studies have shown when people go on a full vegan lifestyle, getting off the cholesterol, they actually have higher brain activity. So going vegan will not only reduce the brain cancer risks, it will increase your abilities to make better decisions.

We feed over 9 Billion Cows!

That's 2 Billion more cows than we have people.

There is really something wrong

with management when they think we need to feed the animals

instead of the humans.

reduce sugar 2

I have yet to find one single thing that sugar does to benefit the body, and there is not a single study showing that sugar has any nutritional benefits whatsoever. Even with these proven facts we have become a nation bombarding ourselves with sugar. It's no surprise that the American health has deteriorated at the exact same time that the sugar consumption has increased.

Today, studies show the average sugar consumption to range between 70 and 150 pounds a year. According to the USDA production numbers, less exports plus imports, in the last 20 years, we have increased sugar consumption in the U.S. 26 pounds to 135 pounds of sugar per person per year! Back in 1900-1905 the average consumption was only 5 pounds per person per year! And coincidentally cardiovascular disease and cancer were virtually unknown a hundred years ago.

This excess of sugar has transformed us into one of the most unhealthy countries on the planet, and sugar is one of the leading causes. Obesity and a great number of other health problems like Type II Diabetes are directly connected to the consumption of sugar. So if you want to live a healthy vibrant life, get off the sugar completely.

Try some stevia, which is a natural plant. And even the dried fruit is far better than any honey, syrup or sugar. I recommend that you stick to the fresh fruits for your sugar fix. Oranges, grapes and strawberries will be far better for you and taste great, especially when your taste buds are working right.

WHAT IS SUGAR?

Sugar is one of the three kinds of carbohydrate; starch, fiber and sugar. Sugar is found in foods of plant origin. In food, sugars are classified as either naturally occurring or added sugar. Naturally occurring sugars include lactose in milk, fructose in fruit, honey and even vegetable sugars.

Added sugars originate from beets, corn, grapes, and sugar cane, which are processed before being added to foods we eat. The body cannot tell the difference between naturally occurring and added sugars because they are chemically similar.

Food sources of naturally occurring sugars also provide vitamins and minerals, while foods containing added sugars provide mainly calories and very few vitamins and minerals. For this reason, the calories in added sugar are generally called "empty calories" or "killer calories" because of their body killing attributes.

NUTRITIONAL FACTS LABELS

On the Nutrition Facts panel of a food label, 'sugars' include both added sugar and naturally occurring sugars for the total sugar in a product. This deception has grouped the unhealthy sugars with the natural sugars. So we have to know how to read the label and know the added sugars.

Generally on the ingredient list, only added sugars are listed such as corn syrup, high-fructose corn syrup, dextrose, maltodextrins, or granulated sugar. So we must read the ingredient list and know what to look for.

reduce sugar 2

Different Sugars: Sugar consumption includes highly refined sugars that are incorporated into many of the foods we eat like bread, peanut butter, condiments, sauces, etc. Some of these are better known as sucrose (table sugar), dextrose (corn sugar), and high fructose corn syrup. There are 4 basic classes of simple sugars; sucrose, fructose, honey, and malts. They are all deemed "harmful" to optimal health when long-term consumption occurs.

Health Issues: Simple sugars have been documented to contribute to health problems, including: asthma, mood disorders, mental illness, nervous disorders, diabetes, heart disease, gallstones, hypertension, and arthritis.

Insulin Impacts: Sugar raises insulin levels, inhibiting the release of growth hormones which depresses the immune system. Too much insulin promotes the storage of fat, so that when you eat foods that are high in sugar, you're enabling rapid weight gain and elevated triglyceride levels, both of which have been linked to cardiovascular disease.

Degenerative Disease: Sugar has no real nutritional value and as a result, has a deteriorating effect on the body systems, causing sugar consumption to be one of the 3 major causes of degenerative disease, and aging.

Cancer Culprits: Turns out that one of cancer's preferred fuel is none other than glucose. Controlling one's blood-glucose levels through diet, exercise, supplements, meditation and prescription drugs – when necessary – can be extremely important to a cancer treatment program.

SUGAR NAMES TO WATCH OUT FOR:

barley malt

beet sugar

dextran

brown sugar

CANE SUGAR

Buttered Syrup

cane-juice crystals

date sugar

CORN SYRUP

carob syrup

caramel

corn-syrup solids

dextrose

diastatic malt

FLORIDA CRYSTALS

d i a s t a s e

ethyl maltol

fructose

evaporated cane juice

fruit juice

fruit-juice concentrate

2 reduce sugar

glucose solids

golden syrup

raw sugar   GOLDEN SUGAR

glucose

grape sugar   honey

Invert Sugar   high-fructose corn syrup

lactose   molasses

MALT SYRUP

maltodextrin

refiner's syrup

maltose

mannitol

sorghum syrup

sorbitol

sucrose

turbinado sugar

yellow sugar

WOW!!! THAT'S A LOT OF HIDDEN SUGAR!

Americans devour over 7.3 billion pounds of candy every year, and spend an estimated $23.1 billion dollars on candy and gum alone. The average American consume a record 27.3 pounds of candy and gum annually, the equivalent of about six regular sized chocolate bars a week. That's just the candy numbers, not including beverages and processed food.

We all know that sugar is one of the main causes of weight gain and obesity. If you just look at the simple labels when it comes to calories, sugars are second only to oil. You see, excess weight comes from excess sugars, excess fat, and excess calories. One tablespoon of sugar contains 45 calories, agave nectar is even higher at 60 calories, and honey is at 65 calories per tablespoon.
That's a huge amount of calories for a little tablespoon of food. Comparative that to an orange which only has 60 calories for the whole orange. Sugars have over 10 times more calories by volume than most any other non refined products.

reduce sugar 2

SUGAR ADDICTIONS:

Sugar is one of the most addictive substances on the planet. In a study with mice, one group of mice were addicted to cocaine and another group was addicted to sugar. When faced with walking over burning hot coals in order to get to their addictions, the cocaine addicted mice would not walk over the hot coals, but the sugar addicted mice would literally burn their feet to get to the sugar.

It's a common phrase: "I'm addicted to sugar." In a study by Princeton University psychologists, they suggest that such urges really may be a form of addiction, sharing some of the physiological characteristics of drug dependency. One university after another are finding the same conclusions. Studies show that "sugar" is just as habit-forming as any narcotic; and its use, misuse, and abuse is one of our nations greatest problems.

SUGAR IS LIKE COCAINE MOLECULES

White refined sugar is not a food. It is a pure chemical extracted from plant sources, purer in fact than cocaine, which it resembles in many ways.

It has 12 carbon atoms, 22 hydrogen atoms, 11 oxygen atoms, and absolutely nothing else to offer. The chemical formula for cocaine is $C_{17}H_{21}NO_4$. Sugar's formula is $C_{12}H_{22}O_{11}$. For all practical purposes, the difference is that sugar is missing the "N", or nitrogen atom.

If you have any doubts as to the detriments of sugar, try leaving it out of your diet for several weeks and see if it makes a difference! You may also notice you have acquired an addiction and experience some withdrawal symptoms.

Knowing
the extreme damage that sugar causes
and becoming more conscious of the physical, mental, and lifestyle
factors that stimulate sugar cravings;
your ability to tame your sweet tooth should be

a piece of cake

—figuratively speaking.

reduce oils 3

Oil is one of those deceptive products that most people do not seem to have a problem with or even think that it is harmful, yet it is one of the leading elements of obesity. A tablespoon of oil contains about 120 calories. Oil is still a refined and processed product that can keep the body from functioning properly. This is including olive oil, coconut oil and any other kind of oil that you can think of. People try to justify that one oil is better than another when in all reality, they're all bad for you, plain and simple! So if you want to get healthier reduce the amount of oil you consume.

The body does need a portion of fat in the diet, with doctors' opinions ranging from 5% on up to 20%. It is a fact that you will get all the fat you need without adding refined and processed oils to your diet. Even an avocado has a full day's supply of fat.

You see we are doing the same thing with the oils that we are doing with the salt. Yes we do need a little, but the whole world has escalated it into a 10 pound per person per month addiction. And this excess of fat causes so many problems like obesity, and heart disease. You see refined and processed oils actually stimulate our own liver to produce more cholesterol.

WHAT ARE OILS?

Quite simply oils are fats. While fats are generally solid at room temperature, oils are liquid. Fatty acids are part of the makeup of fats and oils and it is their structure that decides the flavors, textures and melting points. It is also the fatty acids that decide whether the fat or oil in question is a saturated or unsaturated fat or, in other words, good or bad fat.

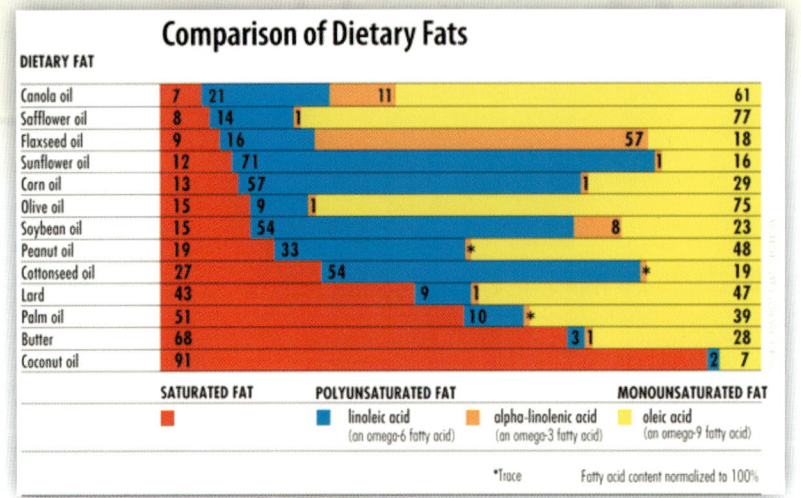

THE COOKING OIL MANUFACTURING PROCESS

Cooking oils are highly processed, using manufacturing methods that are destructive to the oil molecules. These practices are utilized primarily to lengthen and stabilize the shelf life of the oil. After oils are pressed or solvent extracted from seeds and nuts, they are de-gummed, refined, bleached, and deodorized. This process is known as RBD (refined, bleached, deodorized oil). The result of this processing makes the oil become colorless, odorless, and tasteless. What many people don't know is that valuable 'minor ingredients' including antioxidants, phytosterols, chlorophyll, flavor molecules, color molecules, lecithin, and other oil-soluble beneficial molecules are removed too.

Step 1: NaOH is used to remove the natural, alkali-soluble 'minor ingredients' from the oil. These minor ingredients are good for health, but diminish product shelf life and that is why manufacturers choose to remove them from the oil and discard them. NaOH is a very corrosive base used to burn clogged sink and drain pipes open.

Step 2: H_3PO_4, a very corrosive acid used commercially for de greasing windows, is used to remove the acid-soluble 'minor ingredients'. Again, for the sake of longer shelf life, which makes larger market gains, fewer returns due to spoilage, and greater profits, these natural molecules with health benefits are removed.

Step 3: Bleaching clays are used which damage the molecules that give oil its color. Because the color molecules absorb light, and subsequently, the light then damages oil molecules, this process is carried out to obtain greater shelf stability at the expense of health benefits. Unfortunately, bleaching produces rancidity, which imparts bad odor to oils. The rancid oil must then be cleaned up to remove the bad flavor and odor. The oil must be deodorized.

Step 4: Deodorization takes place at frying temperatures (between 220° and 245°C). The bad odors and flavors are removed, and the oil becomes colorless, odorless, and tasteless, but these cooking oils are now palatable and have a long shelf life.

WHAT'S WRONG WITH HEATING OILS?

Trans fat can also occur when good fats are heated. The heating oil starts a process called oxidation which has the same effect as partial hydrogenation and forces the carbon atoms that are joined to other carbon atoms to join with hydrogen atoms instead. This of course makes the oil become more saturated and therefore worse for our health. So you see, we really need to do a lot less frying.

WHAT ABOUT COCONUT OIL?

Coconut oil has been the hot topic lately. Many people are claiming that coconut oil is good for you, and that is just not the case. Of course the coconut manufacturers have done a great job marketing their products as healthy when in fact, it is still fat, it is still 120 calories per tablespoon, and it will still have even greater harmful effects on the body than doing without.

Coconut oil has the highest level of saturated fat and there are some claims that it is a good saturated fat. That's like saying there is a good type of cocaine. While it may not be as bad as other saturated fas, it's still fat, it's still 120 calories per tablespoon, and is still harmful the body. Don't be fooled by the claims developed by the industry in order for them to sell the product.

Coconut oil also claims that it has a higher smoke point, this is at 350 degrees compared to 320 degrees for olive oil. Their claims are that it is better for frying. While this may be true, the difference is relatively insignificant when it comes to general frying because most people fry at a hotter temperature, too hot for even coconut oil. The other element of deep frying is that while a standard deep frying temperature of 350 degrees is preferred, coconut oil is far too expensive for anybody to use in large amounts for deep frying. We must keep in mind the fact that the coconut oil

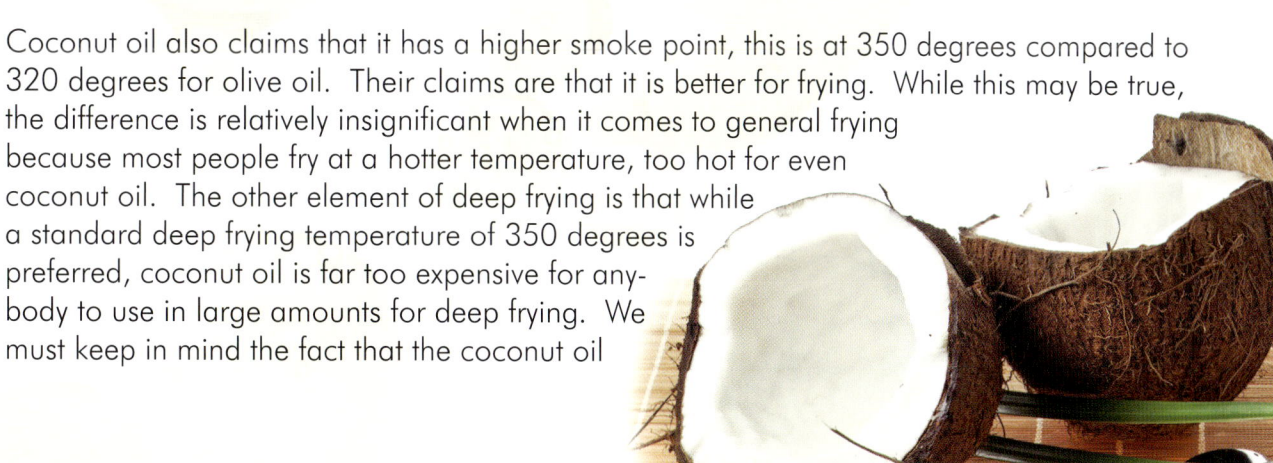

industry is telling us to fry food with their so called better oil, when in fact, fried food is still bad for you. We shouldn't be frying in anything.

At this time, numerous governmental agencies and medical organizations recommend against the consumption of significant amounts of coconut oil due to the high saturated fat content. And while the jury is still out on the health side of coconut oil, it may have better qualities than other oils, but it still has harmful elements too. Some people are saying that the saturated fat is a good saturated fat because it turns to liquid at 72 degrees. Well it's still saturated fat, and coconut oil has been proven to stimulate the liver into producing more cholesterol. So the same conclusion still stands strong, it is not good for you.

It takes over 1,000 pounds of coconut to make one gallon of coconut oil!

Maybe we should just be eating the coconut?

WHAT ABOUT OLIVE OIL?

Olive oil industries have done the same thing getting great success in claims that their products are good for you when in all reality, it's still just a fat, with harmful elements in it. Most of the claims are in the antioxidant values. One of the biggest problems with this, is the fact that most of the oil that gets to America is years after the harvest and most of the antioxidant values have been lost. All of these antioxidant values can also be found in an olive. Now isn't that an amazing discovery?

Olive oil still has a strong reputation and that is not going to change. The biggest problem with this reputation that they have is that the consumers are flocking to olive oil like never before. The justifications for consumption of olive oil has turned into gluttony, and in an ironic way, have actually contributed to the global health problem because of the excessive intake of this still harmful product. The real ticket is moderation, and when it comes to olive oil we need to treat it as any other oil; it's still fat, it's still 120 calories per tablespoon, and it is still harmful to the body when taken in excess.

WHAT ARE THE DIFFERENCES BETWEEN OLIVE OILS?

Extra virgin: Considered the best, this oil comes from the first pressing of the olives.

Virgin: Comes from the second pressing.

Pure: Undergoes some processing, such as filtering and refining.

Extra light: Undergoes considerable processing and only retains a very mild olive flavor.

LET'S LOOK AT SOME OF THE DEFINITIONS OF FATS CONTAINED IN THE OIL WE CONSUME:

Mono-unsaturated Fatty Acid (MUFA): This refers to a healthy fatty acid, which lowers the levels of bad cholesterol and triglyceride without lowering good cholesterol levels.

Polyunsaturated Fatty Acid (PUFA): This lowers the levels of good and bad cholesterol. This is not beneficial as low good cholesterol increases the risk of developing heart disease.

Saturated fats: When consumed in excess, it increases the levels of both the total as well as the bad cholesterol in the blood, thereby allowing fat to be deposited on the walls of the blood vessels. This promotes the formation of blood clots and heart disease.

Unsaturated fats: These are considered good for health as they do not increase the levels of bad cholesterol.

Refined oil: This type of oil has been purified with chemicals to remove any suspended particles, toxic substances, flavor components, color and odor, thereby leaving behind a clear and bland oil.

Filtered oil: Obtained by the traditional cold pressing method, this is filtered once or twice to remove suspended particles.

RICEBRAN OIL - THE ONE TO WATCH

This is the newer oil that I am really interested in keeping a good eye on. As it gains popularity, and because of its inexpensive properties, it will be interesting to see how the world treats it. Will competitive markets try to discredit it in order to secure their own profits like the milk industry does with soy, or like olive oils do to canola? Or will manufacturing companies use its healthy side as a marketing tool for increased sales?

Ricebran oil is a relatively new oil that is extracted from ricebran and is gaining popularity in Asian countries like Japan, Korea, China and India. It is not very expensive and it is high in mono-unsaturated fatty acids and has good cholesterol-lowering properties. It also contains natural vitamin E, which is an antioxidant. It is the ideal cooking oil since it has good stability and is suitable for deep-frying.

HEALTHY COOKING TIPS:

Try doing a water sauté, it's a lot better for you. Some people will even do a 90% water and 10% oil. This will help your reduction of oil and save you a lot of money in the process.

If you're going to have vinegar and oil, go more vinegar and less oil. Another thing you can do for salads is the squeeze of lemon juice, or blend some fruits like berries and oranges with spices.

Many times when a baking recipe is calling for oil, it is to add moisture to the product. You can achieve a great moisture by simply adding a little unsweetened applesauce.

IT'S ALL ABOUT ELIMINATING THE OIL FROM YOUR DIETS. EXCESS OIL, IN YOUR COOKING IS GENERALLY NOT NEEDED.

SALT - FRIEND OR FOE

Salt is an essential part of the body and we will have serious health problems without it, but how bad is this element that we hear so many negative things about? Sodium, one of salts main compounds, is one of the primary electrolytes in the body. All four electrolytes (sodium, potassium, magnesium, and calcium) are available in unrefined salt, as are other vital minerals needed for optimal bodily function. Too little salt in the diet can lead to muscle cramps, dizziness, or electrolyte disturbances, which can cause neurological problems, serious health issues and even death. So why do we only hear how bad salt is for us, and is it really that bad?

The problem in society is that we have such a huge abundance of salt in our dietary lifestyles. This overload of salt can be extremely harmful to our bodies. According to many credible organizations, we should only have 500mg to 1,000mg a day of salt, that is less than 1/2 teaspoon. Yet global studies have shown actual consumption ranging between 2,700mg and 4,900mg a day. That's pushing 10 times more salt than the body should be having, and many people in this world of fast food and junk food are consuming in excess of 50 times the amount of salt they should be having.

An abundance of salt has been linked to a number of health problems including:

Stroke, cardiovascular disease, hypertension or high blood pressure, ulcers, and even death. Yes, too much salt in a quick amount of time has causes many deaths, especially in children.

Today, roughly 65 million Americans have hypertension, or high blood pressure, and another 45 million have pre-hypertension; that's 1 out of 3. Blood pressures greater than 140/90 are considered hypertension, while those between 120/80 and 140/90 are considered to be

pre-hypertension. Ninety percent of Americans will ultimately develop hypertension unless preventive actions are taken, and there are many studies linking salt consumption as one of the main culprits.

Roughly 75 percent of the daily sodium intake of the U.S. population comes from salt in processed and restaurant foods and only 10 percent comes from a natural content in food. In our fast paced world of convenience it is extremely difficult for consumers to follow a low-sodium diet. This is because many canned and frozen foods contain 1,000mg or more of sodium in an eight-ounce serving. Consumers must read food labels very carefully to select lower sodium products. Often such products are difficult to find and cost more to purchase. Restaurant meals, which are not labeled, often contain 3,000mg of sodium or more without the consumer's knowledge.

In all reality, if the only thing you eat is processed foods and restaurant food, you will never ever come close to getting down to the appropriate levels of salt that we should be consuming. Sticking to the whole natural foods in their natural state is the most effective way to get off the astronomical amounts of salt we are consuming.

From one extreme to the other, a lack of salt can cause a desire to overeat and often results in a craving of animal proteins, while too much salt will increase thirst and also trigger cravings for sweet foods. The body naturally craves the products that will compensate for the imbalance created. This is why weight gain is often related to salt consumptions, both too much or too little can result in additional pounds.

We always hear about all the bad elements of salt and not one single time have I ever heard a doctor talk about what a friend salt is in our lives. So I've done some research and compiled a little list of things that salt does to benefit the body.

TOP 10 BENEFITS OF SEA SALT

1. Strengthens Immune System: Salt naturally helps the body build up a strong immune system so that we can fight off fevers, colds, flu, allergies, and other autoimmune disorders.

2. Alkalizing: Salt is alkalizing to the body, it can help you to prevent and reverse high levels of acids in the body, which in turn eliminates the risks for many serious and life-threatening diseases.

3. Weight Loss: Believe it or not, sea salt can also help you in weight loss. It helps the body to create digestive juices so that the foods you eat are digested faster, and it helps to prevent buildup in the digestive tract, which eventually can lead to constipation and weight gain.

4. Skin Conditions: A salt bath can help to relieve dry and itchy skin as well as serious conditions such as eczema and psoriasis. The bath naturally opens up the pores, improves circulation in the skin and hydrates the tissues so that your skin can heal.

5. Asthma: Salt is effective in reducing inflammation in the respiratory system. Thus the production of phlegm is slowed down so that you can breathe easier again. Some say that sprinkling sea salt on the tongue after drinking a glass of water is just as effective as using an inhaler. But the great thing about sea salt is that it has no side effects when taken in moderation.

6. Heart Health: When salt is taken with water it can help to reduce high cholesterol levels, can reduce high blood pressure and help to regulate an irregular heart beat. Salt can actually help to prevent atherosclerosis, heart attacks and strokes.

7. Diabetes: Salt can help to reduce the need for insulin by helping to maintain proper sugar levels in the body. Here, the salt is an essential part of the diet if you are diabetic, or at risk for the disease.

8. Osteoporosis: Over 1/4 of the amount of salt that is in the body is stored in the bones, where it helps to keep them strong. When the body lacks salt and water it begins to draw the sodium from the bones, which then can eventually lead to osteoporosis. Thus by drinking plenty of water and consuming salt in moderation you can prevent osteoporosis.

9. Muscle Spasms: Potassium is essential for helping the muscles to function properly. Salt not only contains small amounts of potassium, but it also helps the body to absorb it better from other foods. This is effective in helping to prevent muscle pains, spasms and cramps.

10. Depression: Sea salt also has shown to be effective in treating various types of depression. The salt helps to preserve two essential hormones in the body that help you to better deal with stress. These hormones are serotonin and melatonin, which help you to feel good, relax and sleep better at night.

Wow, that's a lot of benefits that we just don't hear about. Due to the massive amount of damage that is being done from excessive amounts of salt in our diet, we never see any of the benefit, and yet there are a lot more benefits to salt than we would ever realize. Some are not just aids to our health, they are literally vital for sustaining life. We need salt more than anyone would ever realize.

So you see, salt really is not as bad as people are led to believe. In fact, it is one of the most important elements in our bodies. Some people have no problems with excess salt, while others have huge problems with even a little too much salt. That's why I thought you would like to see both sides of the truth. Salt is good for you and there is no doubt about it, but too much salt is bad for you and not enough salt is really bad for you. The best thing to do is take salt in very low moderation and remove yourself from the 90% who are consuming harmful amounts of salt. Your health really does depend on the decisions that you make. Be smart about your health, do your homework, and act on the knowledge you receive.

When you go on a vegan lifestyle, having no animal products whatsoever, you will not have all that cholesterol and animal fat surrounding all your taste buds. This will enable your taste buds to do the job they are supposed to be doing and you will not need all the salt to flavor your food. You will naturally be lowering your salt consumption to the appropriate levels you should be having.

SEA SALT WARNINGS

The other grand deception is that sea salt is better and healthier for you than any other salt. For the most part, salt is salt. It doesn't matter what claims you hear, there is generally only a slight fractional difference of nutritional value between any of them. According to many credible universities, including the Mayo Foundation for Medical Education and Research, sea salt and table salt have the same basic nutritional value, they are both made up of sodium and chloride. Mayo Foundation and others have claimed that even though sea salt is being marketed as healthier, it's just not the case, their chemical makeup is the same and the only differences are in the flavor and texture. Salt and sea salt have virtually no significant differences.

reduce salts 4

I do recommend the natural kosher and sea salts because they do not have the processing that many of the table salts have and I am a true believer in staying away from any type of processing. I'm not going to recommend sea salt to you because it's better for you.

Being a chef, I use sea salts for the flavor. I get far better flavor out of the natural sea salt than any other salt. I will give you a confession from the kitchen that the restaurant industry really doesn't want you to know. When you use sea salt you can actually use more salt, and your food is not going to taste salty. It is a lot more forgiving in commercial cooking. That's one of the reasons why restaurant foods have much higher sodium contents.

The biggest warning, salt is still salt. The fact is that people are now justifying their salt addictions by their claims that sea salt is healthier when in all reality it is not. It still comes down to the overconsumption of salt and many people in society are now consuming even more salt than they ever have before because of this extremely successful marketing plan. In reality, this bold marketing claim is literally causing far more sickness and death than we ever had before because of the false illusions that it has been created in order to drive sales into their industry.

CONFUSED? IS SALT GOOD OR BAD? THE ANSWER IS BOTH.

Too much salt is bad for you, and too little salt is even worse. In all reality, the best thing we can do is reduce the amount of salt we are consuming, and natural sea salt will still be better than the processed table salt.

TOP 5 TIPS TO AVOID EXCESS SALT

1. Make recipes from scratch: This will help allow you to avoid using too much salt in your diet. Most foods really don't need all the salt in the cooking process. Limes and lemons are good salt substitute in recipes, and there are quite a few salt free flavorings out there.

2. Stay away from the processed food industry: I always say, "eat things that are a plant, not manufactured in a plant". Many of the processed and manufactured foods are amped up with huge amounts of salt.

3. Avoid salting your food: Try zesting, mild spices, and herbs. Lemon and lime juice work great too. Use spices other than salt when cooking. Examples include pepper, basil, thyme, garlic.

4. Make better choices: Choose foods with low sodium like fruits and vegetables. Avoid salty snacks such as pretzels and potato chips.

5. Go Vegan: It's the best way to get your taste buds working the way they should be. Your food will taste so much better without all the salt. Eat more fresh fruits and vegetables.

". . .all of us have in our veins the exact same percentage of salt in our blood that exists in the ocean, and, therefore, we have salt in our blood, in our sweat, in our tears. *We are tied to the ocean.* And, when we go back to the sea. . . we are going back to whence we came."

-John F. Kennedy

eliminate alcohol & drugs

Red Wine contains a significant level of flavonoids and red anthocyanin pigments that act as an antioxidant which protect cholesterol from oxidation, reduce blood lipid levels, and inhibit blood clotting, thereby providing protection against heart disease. Retailers and alcoholics around the world were jumping with joy to think that they could justify this product that is the direct cause of millions of deaths.

The amazing part is that the same properties are derived from the red grape juice and not the alcohol content. You will get the exact same benefits from grape juice and even more nutrients that are not killed by the fermenting process that wine goes through.

The sad truth of this wine discovery is that it enables the industries to promote their products as good for you when in all reality they are extremely bad for you, and it gives the consumers a false sense of purpose to justify their actions even though they know it's not the absolute and total truth.

The bottom line here is that alcohol kills the body, mind and spirit. Some people will continue to justify that wine has a beneficial factor to it, well, so does grape juice, and it doesn't kill thousands of people every year like alcohol does.

SATAN GATHERED THE FALLEN ANGELS TOGETHER TO DEVISE SOME WAY OF DOING THE MOST POSSIBLE EVIL TO THE HUMAN FAMILY. ONE PROPOSITION AFTER ANOTHER WAS MADE, TILL FINALLY SATAN HIMSELF THOUGHT OF A PLAN. HE WOULD TAKE THE FRUIT OF THE VINE, ALSO WHEAT, AND OTHER THINGS GIVEN BY GOD AS FOOD, AND WOULD CONVERT THEM INTO POISONS, WHICH WOULD RUIN MAN'S PHYSICAL, MENTAL, AND MORAL POWERS, AND SO OVERCOME THE SENSES THAT SATAN SHOULD HAVE FULL CONTROL. UNDER THE INFLUENCE OF LIQUOR, MEN WOULD BE LED TO COMMIT CRIMES OF ALL KINDS. THROUGH PERVERTED APPETITE THE WORLD WOULD BE MADE CORRUPT. BY LEADING MEN TO DRINK ALCOHOL, SATAN WOULD CAUSE THEM TO DESCEND LOWER AND LOWER IN THE SCALE.

- ELLEN WHITE

Often, people start drinking alcohol in order to get to sleep. Alcohol is initially a sedative and will encourage sleep. However, alcohol will lead to disrupted sleep, because alcohol has a rebounding effect later in the night. As a result, there is strong evidence linking alcoholism and forms of insomnia. So in order to get a better night's sleep, refrain from any alcohol use.

TOBACCO - A DRUG

Along with the alcohol and drugs is the substance called tobacco that needs to be eliminated. The World Health Organization along with countless other professionals agree that quitting smoking is one of the best things you can ever do to aid in your health.

It is well known that tobacco is addictive, even in the form of chewing tobacco. One of the reasons is because the tobacco industries do the same thing that the food industries do, they make their products as addictive as possible. Cigarettes contain as many as 600 added ingredients including sugar, menthol, and even ammonia.

Nicotine is the primary psychoactive chemical, or drug, in tobacco that makes cigarettes addictive. Statistically every cigarette smoked shortens the user's lifespan by 11 minutes. About half of cigarette smokers die of tobacco-related disease and lose on average 14 years of life. Cigarette use by pregnant women has also been shown to cause birth defects, including mental and physical disabilities.

CIGARETTES ADDICTIVE ADDITIVES

It's kind of ironic that the words "addictive" and "additive" are so closely similar. And amazingly when it comes to food or tobacco or anything we consume, the additives are generally designed to produce more addictive results.

A list of 599 cigarette additives, created by five major American cigarette companies, were approved by the Dept. of Health and Human Services in April of 1994. None of these additives are listed as ingredients on the cigarette packs. Chemicals are added for organoleptic purposes and

eliminate alcohol & drugs

many boost the addictive properties of cigarettes, especially when burned.
One of the major chemicals on the list, is ammonia, which helps convert bound nicotine molecules in tobacco smoke into free nicotine molecules. This process is known as freebasing which enhances the effect of the nicotine on the smoker.

This same thing is done to our food supplies every day. Government allows additives to be put into everything we consume, without our knowledge. As with food, the cigarette additives are designed to make the product more addictive in order for the industry to increase sales; and in effect, the outcome is an increase in sickness and death.

New research has shown that a third hand smoke also causes problems. Third hand smoke is from the residue of cigarette chemicals left on clothes, furniture and carpets after second hand smoke has gone. It has statistically shown to increase the probability of cancer and lung related diseases with people who are in contact with it.

[**WORLD HEALTH ORGANIZATION REPORT**
Smoking causes over 3 million deaths a year and by 2030 that number will be closer to
10 million people a year.]

PRESCRIPTION DRUGS

It really doesn't matter what drug we are talking about, drugs are drugs, and they're all harmful to the body. Even the prescription drugs are still harmful to the body. All you have to do is look at the dozens of side effects that accompany most of them. Now I'm not telling you to quit taking all your prescription medications, but there are ways to eliminate many of those medications simply with proper diet and exercise.

One of the things you will discover is that there are thousands of people out there who are being prescribed medications that they really don't need. I have a real problem with the globally famous phrase "Listen to your doctor". Well what if your doctor is an idiot?

It happens all the time, and the really sad part is that a lot of the doctors are just robots for the pharmaceutical industry. They have a pill for every illness; instead of treating the lifestyle problems that are causing the sicknesses in the first place. These doctors are just not being trained in prevention, and they are certainly not being trained in the reversal of sickness and disease.

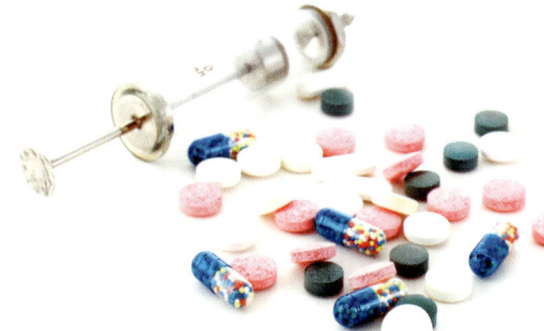

IT'S A REALLY SCARY REALITY WHEN YOU REALIZE THAT WHAT DOCTORS DO, IS CALLED A "PRACTICE"

There are purposes for doctors and we should not be using them as a band-aid to put on a severed jugular vein. It's not treating the cause of the problem to take a pill if you are going to continue to eat such an unhealthy lifestyle. What we eat has the most profound effects on our body, mind and spirit; and what we need to do is just get back to the basics of eating whole natural foods, fresh fruits, and vegetables. It's really not a complicated solution for the biggest health problem facing our planet. Many doctors know this information and most the people are just not listening to them.

[He that takes medicine and neglects diet, *wastes the time of his doctor.*
Ancient Chinese Proverb]

reduce or eliminate caffeine

Coffee is one of the world's most popular drinks. Four out of five Americans drink coffee and consume over *400 million cups a day.*

Serious overdoses of caffeine have been known to cause death and serious reactions requiring hospitalization, and they are occurring from as little as two grams of caffeine. Caffeine has both short term and long term effects that can result in permanent medical problems. Everything from blurred vision to heart attacks have been associated with caffeine.

Caffeine is not just in the coffee, you will find it in many sodas, chocolate, and even certain pain relievers are amped with caffeine.

The food and drug administration once stated that if caffeine were introduced today, it would never be approved for consumption.

Ironically enough, with any harmful element, there is always people finding benefits to justify the addictions. In the case of caffeine, the claims of decreased risk of heart disease and liver disease top the studies. You will also find many benefits of caffeine popping up like increased attentions, memory performance and even weight loss. As many of these claims are still under the microscope and many certainly do have some truth to their claims, it still does not eliminate the extremely harmful effects that are associated with the consumption of caffeine. It's like saying, I would like a bowl of cherries with my cocaine.

Some ADHD sufferers self-medicate with caffeine, reporting a sedative or calmative effect. This may be explained by a low arousal theory of ADHD, which suggests that ADHD sufferers have lower than normal levels of dopamine and arousal, and are driven to seek more intellectual and emotional stimuli from the surrounding environment than people without ADHD in order to compensate. Because caffeine acts as an antagonist to receptors of adenosine, a neurotransmitter that inhibits arousal, ingestion of caffeine may cause the arousal levels of ADHD sufferers to return to normal and alleviate some of the symptoms of the disorder.

Caffeine has many of the same characteristics as its familiar counterparts like morphine and codeine. In large amounts, and especially over extended periods of time, caffeine can lead to a condition known as caffeinism. Caffeinism usually combines caffeine dependency with a wide range of unpleasant physical and mental conditions including nervousness, anxiety, insomnia, headaches, and heart palpitations. Furthermore, because caffeine increases the production of stomach acid, high usage over time can lead to peptic ulcers, erosive esophagitis, and gastroesophageal reflux disease.

There are also four caffeine-induced psychiatric disorders recognized by many specialists, including: caffeine intoxication, caffeine-induced anxiety disorder, caffeine-induced sleep disorder, and caffeine-related disorder not otherwise specified (NOS).

TIPS TO GET OFF CAFFEINE:

Getting off the caffeine from heavy soda or coffee consumption can create headaches and sometimes nausea. Fortunately, these withdrawal reactions are short lived, only lasting a few days. When you are stopping the caffeine, get a good diet, plenty of rest, and exercise helps too.

For some people, it is best to do gradual reductions when it comes to caffeine. A step down method can really help your caffeine dependencies. In very little time, you will get to the point that you really don't need any caffeine at all and in most cases, your will find that you have more energy without the caffeine than you did with it. That's because the caffeine robs your body of the energy that it would use for your everyday activities as well as robbing your body of its ability to maintain higher performing functions.

DECAFFEINATED COFFEE IS NOT REALLY CAFFEINE FREE, IT GENERALLY CONTAINS ABOUT 3 MILLIGRAMS OF CAFFEINE PER CUP.

MOST ENERGY DRINKS ARE AMPED WITH MORE THAN 80MG OF CAFFEINE. MANY ARE LOADED WITH EXCESSIVE AMOUNTS OF SUGAR AND QUESTIONABLE HERBAL SUPPLEMENTS.

7 eat your biggest meal for breakfast

Have you ever noticed that when society is doing something, it's usually something we should not be doing? We need to do the exact opposite of what people in society are doing in so many ways. Especially with our diet and lifestyles!

Most people have their smallest meal for breakfast, a bigger lunch, and an even bigger dinner. We are a lot better off when we have the biggest meal for breakfast, a smaller lunch, and an even smaller dinner. Here we go doing the exact opposite of what society is doing.

In society most people are having a cup of coffee and a power bar loaded with sugar for breakfast. Then they are literally running on an empty tank, so then they will start having bigger meals, with more fat and more sugar to simulate a fullness effect that will not last. Then the biggest meal is for dinner and that's the meal that generally continues into dessert and snacking till it's time to go to bed. So they're getting all this food right before going to bed, only adding to their weight gain. And more than that, is the fact that you will not be able to sleep near as well as you would if you had the smallest meal for dinner.

When we have our biggest meal for breakfast, we will not be hungry all day and we will actually eat a lot less food. When you have nothing for breakfast, you have to have bigger meals, and even bigger meals to catch up with your empty tank, and you end up eating way more food during the day. And here in America we just eat way too much food, so load up on a big breakfast and you will actually eat less.

Having the biggest meal for breakfast will also give you more energy throughout the day. And when you have more energy, you're going to be more active, and this will increase the amount of calories you will be burning, thus helping you lose or maintain your appropriate weight. It is probably one of the best weight loss practices that I could ever recommend.

Another element of having a big breakfast is all the money that you're going to be saving. Not only will you be saving money by eating less throughout the day, you will actually be having your biggest consumption with the least expensive items to consume. Have you ever noticed that lunches are a lot more expensive than breakfast? And if you go out for dinner, it's even more expensive. So having that biggest meal for breakfast will not only help you become skinnier, it will help make your pocketbook fatter.

I will often have oatmeal for breakfast, along with whole grain breads, bananas, nuts, and even dried fruits. For lunches, salads are the best, I love them! Any kind of salad, every kind of salad, there are so many salads, I could have a different one every day of the year. And for dinner, sometimes I just have an orange, or a little brown rice and veggies. Very simple dinner, and very small.

You see when you go vegan and have the biggest meal for breakfast, it will not only save your health and save you money, it will save you a lot of time. Because you're cooking a lot less. The animal consuming lifestyle we are on as a nation takes cooking time. Why should we go through all the work of cooking when God has already done the cooking for us? And by eating a bigger breakfast we will be cooking far less with God's benefits being far greater in more ways than one.

drink plenty of water

Water water everywhere, but not a drop to drink. At least that's the way many people in today's culture are living their lives. It has been told to us for years how important it is to drink six to eight glasses of water a day and yet this is probably the most neglected of any health advice we have. 6 to 8 cups is old school thinking, but it is still pretty good. The new formula for getting the right amount of water is 1 ounce for every 2 pounds. A 200 pound person should have 100 ounces a day. Ironically, drinking water is the easiest, and least expensive thing you could ever do to maintain a healthy lifestyle.

Water is an absolute necessity for the body and when we are consuming the right amount of water regularly, our bodies function properly. Think of it as the motor oil for an engine. If there is no oil in the engine, it will burn up in no time at all. Well the same thing goes for the human body, without water lubricating every one of the thousands of moving parts, we will simply burn up. So simply drink more water and live a much healthier life.

The choice of an unhealthy nation is to go for the soda, coffee, tea, or power drink. We are now accustomed to purchasing carbonated and caffeinated beverages to the extent of over 2 trillion dollars a year, and even though the bottled water industry has bloomed, it is still just a fraction of the total consumption of beverages.

Old school recommendations would teach us to drink 8 glasses of water a day and there are millions of people out there who do not even drink one. They are literally dying of dehydration and don't even know it. When people go for a fruit juice or tea instead of water to quench their thirst, it is not the same as going for a fresh glass of water. In fact research has shown that women who consume large quantities of beverages other than water actually increase their risk of a fatal heart attack by 2 1/2 times, and men increase their risk by 50%. It is still the water that we need for our body to function properly.

THE HARMFUL EFFECTS RESULTING FROM DEHYDRATION:

- Tiredness
- Migraine
- Constipation
- Muscle cramps
- Irregular blood-pressure
- Kidney problems
- Dry skin
- 20% dehydrated – Risk of death

Harvard School of Public Health
Men who drink plenty of water a day are
50% less likely to develop bladder cancer
as those who only drink a glass a day.

Fred Hutchinson Cancer Research Center, Seattle Washington
Women who drink more than five glasses of water a day
reduce the risk of colon cancer by 45%

drink plenty of water

You lose 1 1/2 cups of water a day just through normal breathing. You lose 1 to 2 cups of water through your skin in normal, non-exercising, low heat temperatures. It is very easy to dehydrate yourself, and can happen in no time at all. Yet it can take anywhere from hours to days to return to a completely rehydrated body again. I have often done huge events in the desert of Las Vegas and found myself so dehydrated that it took me a week to recuperate.

[**EXPERTS RANK WATER SECOND ONLY TO OXYGEN AS** *essential for life.*]

The functions of water for the human body are vital. We can survive many days without food, but very little time without water. Every cell in our body needs water. From head to toe, water is an essential element. Here are just a few of the basic functioning benefits of water.

- Transports nutrients and oxygen to the cells
- Regulates our body temperature
- Moisturizes the air in lungs
- Protects our vital organs
- Helps our organs to absorb nutrients better
- Detoxifies our entire body
- Protect and moisturizes our muscles and joints
- Helps with metabolism

We should also not be waiting until we are thirsty to be drinking this life giving water. Studies have shown that if you are experiencing thirst, you are already in the primary stages of dehydration. When you are going to be conducting higher physical activity, it is best to consume additional water prior to and frequent additional waters through your exercises, and also conduct a replenishing process afterwards.

Drink water to lose weight - Not drinking enough water can make you fat. When you don't drink enough water, your body secretes a hormone called aldosterone This hormone causes tissues to hold on to almost every molecule it possibly can, and this causes your body's fat deposits to increase.

In an amazing study of people who are overweight, it was discovered that they drink a lot less water. Many claimed their restrictions were brought on by trying to reduce water retention and lose weight. Even though water has no sugar, no fat, and no calories, they were still thinking that it added to weight gain. And in other studies, it has actually been proven that adequate water consumption helps lose weight. Drinking water increases your metabolic rate by an average of 30%.

Our bodies consist of 70% water and some organs are in excess of 90%.

- Muscle consists of 75% water

- Brains consists of 90% of water

- Blood consists of 83% water

- Even bones consists of 22% water

When our bodies do not get enough water, the body's natural defense systems are activated. The most vital organs will actually rob water from the other organs, skin, and bones in order to function. This stress from dehydration results in arthritis, kidney stress and failures, premature aging, and a good number of other health problems.

There are many short term symptoms of dehydration such as light-headedness, fatigue, dry mouth and confusion. And the signs of long term dehydration can be so subtle until its too late to repair the damage that has been done. Signs like medical dryness to the skin or mucous membranes, weight gain or loss, subtle stomach pains, muscle loss or pain, can be easily overlooked for one reason or another and may actually be the result of long term water dehydration. Most people don't realize how easy it is to become dehydrated, just a day or two of mild dehydration can result in long term damages.

SYMPTOMS OF DEHYDRATION

• Thirst: Thirst is the most obvious sign that you're already dehydrated. It is always a good practice to drink more water before you experience thirst, don't wait until you're thirsty.

• Hunger: One of the first signs of dehydration is hunger because the food we eat is the body's main source of water. Most people mistake hunger as the indication to eat more, whereas in actual fact, you may be dehydrated and just need water. So before you eat more calories, grab a glass of water instead.

• Dry Skin: Skin is the largest body organ and requires its share of water. If you're hot without sweating, it's a sure sign that you need water fast!

• Dark Urine: Urine is generally pale yellow to clear when you have sufficient water intake. Dark color or strong smell indicates that you need to drink more water.

• Fatigue: General physical and mental stress is a sign that your body is running low on it's water supply.

We know that dehydration happens all the time and every summer it takes the lives of those who are dehydrated. When something as simple as drinking a glass of water can save your life, it seems ironic that hundreds of people die every year from dehydration.

The main reason for this is because dehydration can really sneak up on you, and you are dehydrated before you know it. And when it comes to older people, their thirst sensations are much lower and their need for consistent water is greater. In fact, severe dehydration is one of the primary reasons for elderly hospitalization. In people age 85 and older who are hospitalized for dehydration, 18% will die within 30 days regardless of treatment. It really is so easy to become dehydrated.

I actually try to be consistent with my water drinking. In the morning the best way to start the day is to drink a couple of glasses of water. I don't drink a lot of cold water, room temperature works just fine for me. I also drink a couple glasses of water between each meal. And the only time I don't drink water is with my meal. I will have a glass before I begin to eat, but digestive systems will work a lot better if you drink little or no water with your meal. Give your body a little time to digest its food before drinking any water. Most people are washing their food down and that is not good for us. In fact, in today's world of rush rush, most people are eating on the run so they have to drink with their meal so that they can get it down quicker. Thus the entire digestion system and salivary glands just don't work as efficiently.

Another interesting point about drinking water instead of other beverages involves our teeth. Most of us know that we should not be snacking between meals, but what most people don't realize is that our teeth need to sweat between meals. When we are drinking coffee, tea or sodas, it actually closes the pores of our teeth and increases the development of cavities . So stick to the water and water only between meals.

Drinking a abundant amount of water is vital to your health. You can never imagine just by changing this simple step, you gain tremendous health benefits, and sometimes you can even throw away your migraine medicine or pain killer.

CARDIOVASCULAR DISEASE & WATER MIRACLE:

If you want to do something that is going to significantly

reduce your risk of heart disease, drink water!

Studies of men who drink more than five, 8oz. glasses of water a day have reduced their risk by 46%. And women, the risk was reduced by 59%.

MARK'S TOP 10 HEALTH BENEFITS OF DRINKING WATER

1. Lose Weight: Water has zero calories. Drinking water also reduces hunger, it can also suppress your appetite so you'll eat less. Plus, drinking water helps you lose weight because it boosts your metabolism. This also helps in digestion to move fats and harmful waste particles through your system.

2. Look Younger with Healthy Skin: You'll look much younger when your skin is properly hydrated. Skin is the largest organ we have. Water helps to replenish skin tissue, moisturizes skin and increases skin elasticity.

3. Boost Your Immune System: Drinking plenty of water helps fight against flu and other ailments like kidney stones and even heart attack, respiratory disease, intestinal problems, rheumatism and arthritis. It really is a great tool to keep us from getting sick.

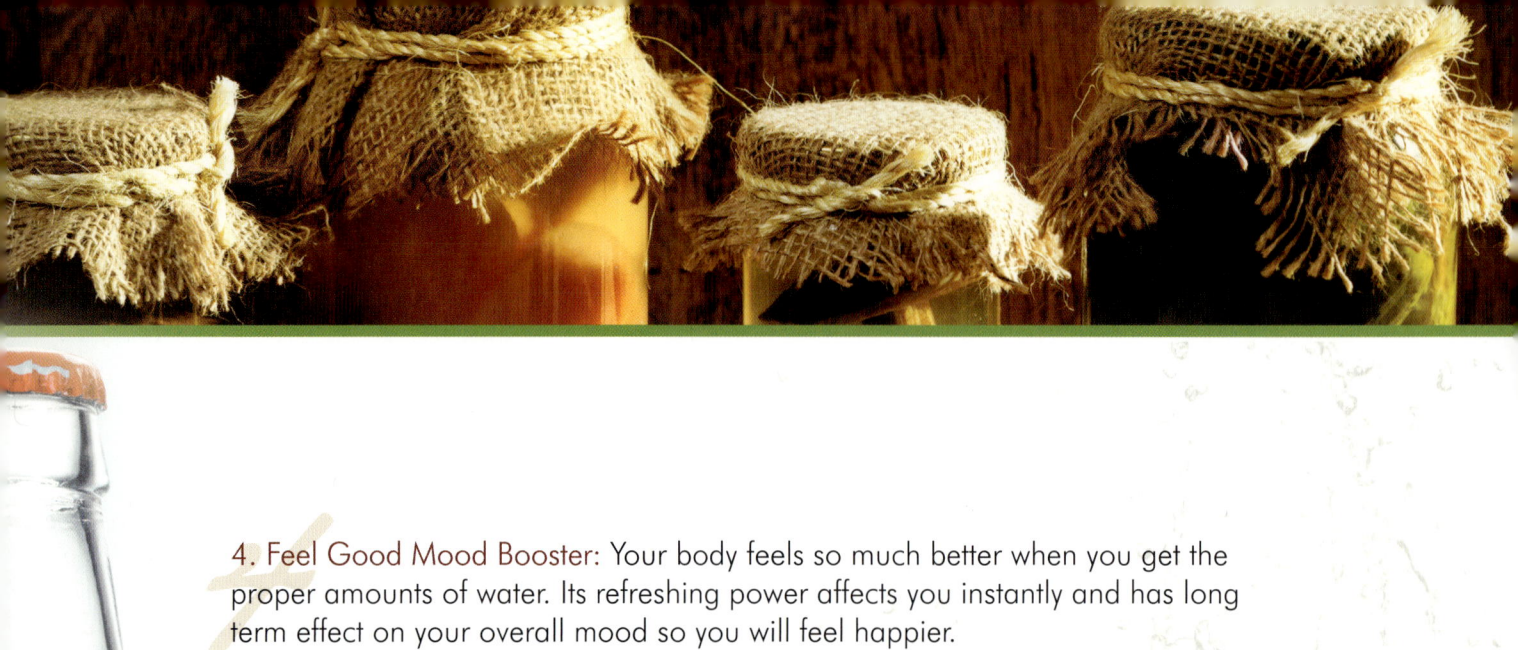

4. Feel Good Mood Booster: Your body feels so much better when you get the proper amounts of water. Its refreshing power affects you instantly and has long term effect on your overall mood so you will feel happier.

5. Better Work Productivity: Your brain is made up of 90% water, and drinking water helps your brain function better. You will think better, be more alert and have more concentration.

6. Better Exercise: You'll feel more energetic when drinking water. It regulates your body temperature and aids your muscles when doing exercises.

7. Helping Headaches: Water helps to relieve headache and back pains due to dehydration. Although there are many other reasons that contribute to headaches, dehydration is the common one and water is a natural pain reliever.

8. Reduces Cramps and Sprains: Proper hydration helps keep your muscles and joints lubricated, so you'll be far less likely get cramps and sprains.

9. Relieves Fatigue: Water is used to help flush out toxins and waste products from your body. If your body lacks water, vital organs will rob water from other organs, muscles, skin and bones and this will cause great fatigue on your entire body and mind.

10. Reduce the Risk of Cancer: Water is a purification system for the body to aid in the removal of harmful particles, toxins and cancer cells. The body's natural purification system is severely disrupted when one does not drink enough water.

exercise regularly

Research suggests that physical activity can reduce the risk of many adverse health conditions, such as coronary heart disease, type II diabetes, osteoporosis, stroke, and even some cancers. In addition, physical activity can help reduce risk factors for conditions such as high blood pressure and even high blood cholesterol. Most researchers agree that even the smallest amount of physical activity is better than none, and greater health benefits can be received by increasing the frequency, intensity, and duration of physical activity.

Only 31 percent of U.S. adults claim that they engage in regular physical activity at least three times per week. About 40 percent of adults report no leisure-time physical activity. About 35 percent of high school students report that they participate in 60 minutes or more of physical activity on 5 or more days of the week, and only 30 percent of students report that they attend physical education class daily. As children get older, participation in regular physical activity decreases dramatically.

EXERCISE CAN HELP YOU:

Burn calories and lose weight

Feel better and have more energy

Live longer, healthier, happier

Reduce risk for many diseases

[PLEASE NOTE:
Check with your doctor before starting any new exercise program. **]**

Having a moderate exercise program has been linked with improved cognitive performance in Alzheimer's disease,

and helps improve memory

and brain function in the elderly.

There are two basic types of voluntary muscle fibers: slow twitch and fast twitch. Slow twitch muscles contract for long periods of time but with little force while fast twitch muscles contract quickly and powerfully but fatigue rapidly.

Slow twitch muscles are for endurance and aerobic exercises and need lots of oxygen to develop. They don't build up a lot of bulk muscle, but they do burn a lot of calories. Running, swimming, and biking are all good forms of exercising those slow twitch muscles.

Fast twitch muscles are the muscles that increase strength. Weight training generally focuses on these types of muscles. When we conduct strength training with our muscles, the muscles are actually learning to enlarge in the event that these muscles will be needed again.

It is actually best to have an exercise training program that will include both types of muscle development.

exercise regularly

[The sovereign invigorator of the body is exercise, and of all exercises *walking is the best* -Thomas Jefferson]

HEALING POWERS OF EXERCISE

1. Studies have shown that exercise helps reverse diabetes as well as preventing diabetes in the first place. Studies also show that exercise has an immediate and prolonged effect on blood sugar amounts among diabetics.

2. Osteoporosis can be aided both in prevention and reversal by weight bearing exercises. Studies also show that balanced weight training routines help build bone density.

3. Strokes have been significantly reduced by exercise in countless studies. In fact just walking 12 miles a week decreases the risk of stroke by as much as 30%.

4. Arthritis patients have received considerable relief from a consistent and moderate exercise program. People with osteoarthritis have discovered decreased pain and increased flexibility with a simple exercise routine.

5. Cardiovascular disease has shown the greatest results of prevention by a consistent exercise program. Even just walking has proven to decrease heart disease by over 20% and running an hour a week has shown reductions as much as 50% in different demographics.

6. Cancers across the board are significantly decreased by exercise programs. In men, prostate cancer reduced 75%, colon cancer reduced 60%. For women, breast cancer reduced 35%. This is just a fraction of the cancers that are literally eliminated by exercise. Studies also show that the frequency of exercise is directly related cancer prevention.

7. Obesity is of course one reason why people exercise, and it can aid greatly in weight loss. I do want to remind you that your calories in must still be lower than your calories out. Many people tend to eat more when they exercise, thus resulting in no weight loss. Also remember that muscle is much heavier than fat, so you might not be losing weight on the scale but your fat loss and muscle gain is worth it.

MENTAL STABILITY

Researchers at the National Institute of Mental Health discovered that regular exercise reduces stress and anxiety. They concluded that exercise has long term relief for depression, and stress hormones. So if you want to feel better mentally, get healthier physically.

Muscle training helps you lose weight.

This is because muscle burns more calories than fat.

It is probably why men have an easier time losing weight than women do. Women who do some strength training actually have far better results.

get plenty of rest

There are multiple theories proposed to explain the function of sleep. When asked why we need sleep, William Dement the founder of Stanford University's Sleep Research Center, answered, "As far as I know, the only reason we need to sleep that is really, really solid, is because we get sleepy." Funny as it sounds, it is a known fact that not everything is known.

It has been pointed out that if sleep was not essential by animals one would expect to find animals that do not sleep at all. We would also find animals that do not need recovery sleep when they stay awake longer than usual and we would find animals that suffer no serious consequences as a result of lack of sleep. Other than a few basal animals that have no brain or a very simple one, no animals have been found that do not need sleep. Some varieties of sharks, such as hammerheads and great whites, must remain in motion at all times to move oxygenated water over their gills, but they still perform "sleep" by deactivating one cerebral hemisphere at a time.

There is nothing more important to developing a healthy lifestyle than a good night's sleep. It helps you make better decisions in everything you do in life. You will make better decisions about what you should be eating which in turn will help you sleep even better. You see it is a big cycle and this balance all starts with a good night's sleep. My mom used to say every hour before midnight is like 2 hours after. Naps are good too, they allow your blood pressure to get back to a normal rate of manageability. It's all about balance and a great balanced life starts with well balanced rest.

MARK ANTHONY'S BEST TIPS TO SLEEP BETTER:

1. Be consistent: Have the same sleep times every night. I am an early to bed and early to rise person that likes to be in bed by 9pm, and I am often up at 4am. On my tours, I am generally in bed by 11pm and get up at 6am-ish. It takes me no time at all to adjust to another consistency. But that is the key word, consistency.

2. Environment: The environment needs to be the most peaceful place possible. I start with having a dark room without lights shining through windows. I like a cool room, but not too cold. Sounds can also be a problem, I had one time where this night bird would be chirping all night, drove me crazy. I solved it by using a fan for a consistent sound and it really works, now I use a fan all the time. Also, use blankets that are comfortable for you, I have my favorites for every season.

3. Shut off the cell phones and technology: I never have any type of equipment on that will wake me up. Shut those phones off! If the planet blows up, you will hear about it tomorrow. If there is a death in the family, they will still be dead tomorrow. If someone has an emergency, they can call 911. I just don't think that there is anything on this earth worth losing a minute's sleep over.

I also don't want the light from the clock bothering me so I have a clock that you have to push a button for it to light up. But in the night, if I wake, I don't look at it because that knowledge puts a limit on the time I have left to sleep and then I can't get back to sleep. Too many people just look at the clock too much and are pressuring themselves to try and sleep.

4. Eating and Water: Don't eat before you go to bed. It is actually best to have your smallest meal for dinner and to have your last food consumption hours before you go to sleep. This really helps your sleeping habits. I also try to drink a bit of water before I go to bed. This is a balance that you want to drink enough so that you will not wake up thirsty while at the same time not drinking so much that you will have to wake up to go to the bathroom. I am really in tune on this and find that if I drink about one cup it works great for me.

5. No Chemicals Stimulants or Depressants: It doesn't matter what you may think you need, you will always pay the price. Some people will take alcohol in order to get to sleep and initially it is a sedative, but alcohol has a rebounding effect a few hours later that will totally rob your restful night's sleep. Alcohol has actually been linked to some forms of insomnia. Caffeine and other stimulants will certainly keep you from getting a good night's sleep too, and even tobacco products have been found to disrupt total sleep time. You are better off staying away from everything. Just go to sleep and get your body into the habit of a better night's sleep.

6. For the graveyard workers: I have worked graveyard for years in different times of my life and the best advice I can give you is to get another job. LOL. Now in all seriousness, I always had a blacked out room, completely blacked out, I went to bed from 11:00am to 7:00pm every day. Even though I got off work at 6:00am, I would sometimes come home and rest or nap for 30 minutes which would help get the blood pressures back to normal, then I would stay up for the rest of the morning until that 11:00am bedtime. On my days off, I kept the same sleep time too. Just a day of change can mess up your whole week, so find the time that works best for you and stick to it. Quite often I would go to the health club at 9:00pm before I went to work, and that works great too. It's all about forming habits and sticking to them.

sunlight and air

People really underestimate the power of sunlight, and with all the cases of skin cancer it's no wonder that more and more people are choosing to abstain from the healing energies that God has provided us in the most miraculous ways. In all reality the world is looking at the healing rays of sunlight as harmful rays of destruction.

Skin cancer claims about 2,000 Americans every year and yet the scientific research indicates that moderate and regular exposure to sunlight can actually prevent thousands of cases of skin cancer each year. Studies have shown that people who regularly receive sunlight actually have lower rates of skin cancer than those who only get out in the sun on rare occasions.

VITAMIN D

Some of the research indicates that the vitamin D we receive from the sunlight is a preventive nutrient. Sunlight vitamin D has been known to decrease colon cancer by up to 80% and actually stops a huge range of cancer cells from growing including skin cancer.

Beyond the cancers, sunlight has been linked to large reductions of osteoporosis and bone cancers. Multiple Sclerosis mortality rates have had up to 75% reductions in mortality rates with moderate sunlight exposures.

One of the biggest advantages to sunlight is in the production of serotonin in the body. Serotonin can also be achieved by eating excessive amounts of refined carbohydrates, ice cream, snack and other high calorie and fat feel good foods. But when you are getting your serotonin from the sun, the cravings for junk foods decreases. This can be a big advantage to the obesity epidemic that the world is experiencing today. Vitamin D has also been directly connected to the reduction of obesity. And when it comes good levels of vitamin D, kidney functions are significantly higher.

Most scientific studies recommend our exposure to sunlight should be 15 to 30 minutes of sunlight 3 times a week. These factors can be dramatically changed by the time of the year,

angle of the sun, and weather conditions. Even in overcast skies we get levels of vitamin D thru the clouds. The other factor is skin types because the darker your skin, the more sunlight you will need. If you have light to fair skin, and burn easily, you may want to start with 5 to 10 minutes a day and work up from there. The National Institute of Health reports that it does take 10 to 15 minutes of sunlight for the synthesis of Vitamin D to occur.

The fact of the matter is that you will not get too much vitamin D from overexposure to the sun. With overexposure you can experience dry skin, premature aging, and we also must keep in consideration the dehydration process. So if you are planning an extended day in the sun, hydrate yourself often. On another note when it comes to sunscreen protection, anything over an SPF of 8 actually blocks out the rays that produce vitamin D.

Today, over 90% of Americans are deficient in vitamin D, in spite of the fact that it's free! People with vitamin D deficiencies have a 25% greater chance of premature death.

Animal milk actually has very little vitamin D in it. 85% of the vitamin D in milk is actually fortified from sources other than milk. This fortified D vitamin has been shown to not easily be absorbed into the body. People think they're getting all the vitamin D they need from milk because of the extreme marketing of this billion dollar industry, but in all reality, it is not an effective source of vitamin D.

Many people are also taking vitamin D supplements, but because vitamin D is fat-soluble, any excess is stored in the body for later use. This excess from the supplement form can cause serious health problems including, depression, fatigue, confusion and a handful of other symptoms.

So when it comes to where we get vitamin D, sunlight is still the best. Getting yourself plenty of sunlight will also help you get a good night's sleep. It also makes you look pretty good and that can certainly help your self-esteem. Any way you look at it, it's a win win in every form under the sun!

BREATHING BETTER

Even though breathing is an innate action, there are a couple things we can do to breathe better. Breathing should expand the lower lungs, this is accomplished by relaxing the abdominal muscles when inhaling. This expands both lower and upper lungs, resulting in better lung function. Another practice is to be taking deep breaths. Seniors have had great success with better lung functions by taking some deep breathing exercises, because they very often never get that oxygen in their lower lungs. A good practice can be to take 5 to 10 deep breaths, hold for a couple seconds, then release and repeat.

DEEP BREATHING

Deep breathing relieves headaches, stomachaches, backaches and releases endorphins, which are natural mood enhancers.
The deep breaths can reduce blood pressure and is also a

great stress reliever.

FRESH AIR REALLY IS BETTER

Fresh air can often be rich in negative ions, especially in sunlight, rain, forests, mountains, and after thunderstorms. These negative ions are good for your body, so take a walk and you will feel invigorated.

It is also recommended to air out your house daily. Bring in that fresh outdoor air. If you have pollen problems or you are in a high smog area, air out the house at night or first thing in the morning. There are air purifiers available that can help reduce particles in the air, just remember that all those particles in the air are not always harmful.
Generally speaking, the air outside is far better than the air inside. Indoor air accumulates a particulate matter that can be over 5 times more polluted than the air outdoors, causing many health problems.

AIR POLLUTION CAUSES CARDIOVASCULAR DISEASE

Studies have shown a 30% increase in mortality from heart diseases when people live close to high pollution areas like freeways and busy city roads. HEPA filtration filters have shown an improvement of 8% in the microvascular blood flow.

DON'T FORGET THE OXYGEN IN THE BLOOD

When we have the right amount of oxygen in the blood, it removes harmful particles and cancer cells. But when our blood is coated with cholesterol and animal fat, it can not remove these killer elements. So eat vegan, with no animal products whatsoever, and your blood will then get the right amount of oxygen it needs.

POLLUTION KILLS

California alone has over 17,000 deaths a year due to air pollution, and globally, over 1.4 billion people live in

unsafe air pollution areas.

THE BRAIN AND AIR

The brain needs a constant flow of oxygen. If you are getting the right amounts of oxygen, you will feel better, have less depression or anxiety, and even think better. On the flip side, the lack of quality air will affect the brain before any other organ. Fainting and dizziness are first signs of poor oxygen levels.

pray every day
12

The last and most important element of health is to stay in prayer; it is the foundation of all health. Body, mind, and spirit are all connected and when we get a deeper connection with God, it will help us make the better decisions in everything we do.

I often tell people to pray for discernment, because that is where we get godly wisdom. It's like using God's eyes instead of your own, God's heart instead of your own, God's mind instead of your own. It's like instead of getting parents intuition, you get godly intuition, and that's what helps you make those right decisions in everything you do.

Prayer is actually the most important thing you could ever do. Daily prayer helps you get balance in your life, helps you make better decisions, and builds a closer relationship with Christ. There is nothing else you could ever do on this planet that will compare to prayer, and beyond the health side is the mental and spiritual side that will grow.

I pray for at least fifteen minutes every morning. Fifteen minutes a day is less than one percent of your day, and if you will just spend one percent of your day, every day, with Christ, He will change your life. It doesn't happen overnight, you have to be consistent. And with your consistent growth in Christ will come the consistent depth of knowledge and the consistent blessings that God has in-store for you.

Of course Satan will try to attack you and disrupt the relationship that you are developing, but stay focused on Christ through anything.

[**ROMANS 8:28**
All things work towards God's greater good to those
who love Him]

Body - Mind - Spirit
IT'S ALL CONNECTED

It's really all about balance and doing the right things. Take one step at a time and continue in the direction of getting healthier. Don't stop on the path! If you run into a stumbling block, turn it into a stepping stone and continue in the right direction.. That is the ONLY way to get results and accomplish ANYTHING in life.

CONTINUED STEPS IN THE RIGHT DIRECTION

Just because you don't know what to pray doesn't mean not to pray. Come to God in silence and listen. We really should spend more of our prayer time listening than we do talking. And just a reminder that one of the definitions of the word listen, is obedience. We must not just listen with our ears, we must listen with our actions.

God's ability to aid and bless us abundantly is limited to our sinful ways, sinful bodies, and sinful natures. Change your sinful ways, and He will bless you beyond measure. Start with asking for forgiveness, and seeking God's direction.

For everyone that asks receives, and anyone that seeks shall find and he that knocks it shall be open. The Greek translation says, "Keep on asking, keep on seeking, and keep on knocking."

"Get on the path," is mentioned more than 100 times in the Bible. I think God is telling us to get on the path.

12 pray every day

It's not enough to just know God's word;
you have to live it, you have to obey it, and you have to love it.
BECAUSE WE KNOW THAT GOD

knows what is best for our lives.

Time alone with the Lord is more precious than anything we could ever possess. It is the ultimate fellowship and the key to the growth and power that only He can provide.

If any of you lack wisdom, let him ask of God, that giveth to all men liberally, and upbraideth not; and it shall be given him.   James 1:5

"Blessed is the man who trusts in the Lord, and whose hope IS the Lord. For he shall be like a tree planted by the waters, which spreads out its roots by the river and will not fear when heat comes; but its leaves will be green, and will not be anxious in the year of drought, nor will cease from yielding fruit." Jer 17: 7-8

"If you turn your foot from the Sabbath, from doing your pleasure on My Holy Day, and call the Sabbath a delight, the Holy Day of the Lord honorable, and shall honor Him, not doing your own ways, nor finding your own pleasure, nor speaking your own words, then you shall delight yourself in the Lord; and I will cause you to ride on the high hills of the earth." Isaiah 58:13-14

Even though I am imperfect in my prayer, I may bow down before the Lord knowing that He understands and that His Holy Spirit will bring me into a better, deeper, more in line prayer life with Him.

MARK ANTHONY'S MESSAGE

Keep well balanced! Diet and exercise, rest & prayer, are all so very important. Spend some time exploring God's great earth, laugh and have fun. Too many times we find ourselves getting bogged down from the world's problems and doom, yet God wants us to have joy and happiness. He has great things in store for us for all eternity, and it all starts right now. Walking with Christ daily will give us every single thing we will ever need.

The easiest and best thing you can do is stick to those whole natural foods. Stick to those foods that don't have an ingredient list. Fresh fruits and vegetables, whole grains and oats are far better for you than any manufactured foods.

Eat a variety of foods and color your plate like a rainbow. God has gifted us with hundreds of different foods and variety is very important. Some people get stuck on the same food every single day, and end up with deficiency problems, so enjoy trying new flavors.

Get Christ involved in your life. Walk with Him and listen to His directing. It is a foundation that needs to be developed for constant growth. Far too often I see people who think they know everything and have stopped their growing process far short of the true walk they should be taking with and in Christ.

I always tell people, take life one step at a time. You don't have to do everything all at once, but you do need to keep taking those steps. The first step is to get off the cholesterol. Just start with a first step, get off that milk and cheese. Then take another step, and one step at a time, day by day, in no time at all, you will be back to living that healthy vibrant life that God wants you to have. He has given us His health message & He wants us to follow it, because He loves us and wants to see us healthy.

Blessings,

Mark Anthony

TABLE OF CONTENTS

STATION SIMPLICITY

Oatmeal Station | 67
Salad Station | 69
Beans, Rice & Pasta Station | 73
Spice Station | 75

RECIPES SIMPLICITY

Breakfast Simplicity | 81
Oatmeal Simplicity | 99
Granola Simplicity | 109
Gourmet Bar Simplicity | 117
Pancake and Waffle Simplicity | 123
Beverages & Blending Simplicity | 133
Salad Simplicity | 141
Salad Dressing Simplicity | 151
Soup Simplicity | 159
Crock-pot Simplicity | 173
Sauce Simplicity | 181
Appetizer Simplicity | 197
Dips and Salsa Simplicity | 201
Hummus Simplicity | 207
Bruschetta Simplicity | 213
Grilling Simplicity | 221
Sandwich Simplicity | 233
Burger Simplicity | 241
Side Simplicity | 257
Entree Simplicity | 269
Stuffing Stuff Simplicity | 279
Dessert Simplicity | 293

EXTRA EXTRA

3ABN Cooking Program Recipes | 329
Index | 389

station simplicity

The easiest way to develop your kitchen into an efficient area of the home is to implement the "STATION" concept. Most people's kitchens are so unorganized that they often run into a couple problems. Some kitchens are so packed with stuff, that they are unable to find anything. And more often than not, the cupboards are filled with food that is so outdated it is unable to be consumed, or it's filled with bugs.

When you develop this Station Mentality, it will make your kitchen life so much simpler. Some people have an area for all their spices, that would be your spice station, so we are going to take this mentality throughout your entire kitchen. One station at a time, we will develop your kitchen into a healthy environment of great tasting foods at every corner.

It seems like the longer we are in a home, the more clutter we get. And when it comes to the kitchen, the more complicated it becomes. The bigger the family, the greater possibilities for complications. Many times we give into our children's desires, filling our homes with tons of unhealthy products from the cries of a child who is unable to make good decisions on their own. This is very sad, because we are actually teaching our children how to live, or rather die by the foods they eat. We need to take a stand! By only having healthy products in our homes, it will ensure that our families will have no other choice but to consume healthy items, and develop the habits that will stay with them for a lifetime.

Your first project is to clear out everything in your home that is unhealthy, and throw it away. I hear a lot of people crying about not wanting to throw it away, wasting good food, or whatever. Well, I have news for you, it's not good food, that's why you're throwing it away! Don't give that garbage to your neighbor for them to be unhealthy, just throw it away. The process of actually throwing it away will also reinforce your abilities to resist purchasing that product again. We don't want to be throwing our hard earned dollars away; well, that's exactly what you're doing every time you buy that unhealthy food at the supermarkets.

Now that you're done clearing your kitchen of all the bad foods, it's time to fill it with lots of great healthy foods that your family will love. And fill it up, it's just food. Buy lots of cans and goods that won't quickly spoil. Have plenty of choices at home so you won't have that complaint that there is nothing to eat. Filling up your kitchen will also keep you from going back to the junk foods of the past, because you won't have room to put it.

I AM GOING TO WALK YOU THROUGH A COUPLE STATIONS THAT ARE AN ABSOLUTE NECESSITY TO ORGANIZING YOUR KITCHEN. YOU WILL ABSOLUTELY LOVE THESE!!!

oatmeal station

Oatmeal Stations are very easy to set up. It is best to take two cupboards rather than one, this way you will have plenty of room for lots of great selections. I like to have a couple different type of oats and granolas. Most of the store bought granolas are filled with sugars too; you can certainly find the healthier ones or actually make your own, and then keep that in your Oatmeal Station.

It is also nice to have a couple containers with premixed combinations of whole grains for crock-pot breakfast cereals. I often turn on the crock-pot right when I go to bed, fill it with the right combinations of rice, whole wheat and water, then my breakfast is ready when I wake.

Beyond the dry cereals, grains and oats, I also have containers with different nuts and dried fruits. I usually get about eight clear airtight containers just for the nuts and dried fruit. They are visually appealing and keep the products fresh.

Sweeteners are a good thing to have in this station too, but remember to use them in very small amounts.

When it comes to the spices, I keep these particular spices in the Oatmeal Station. I want to make the station attractive and convenient without searching everywhere trying to find the products I need. It's okay to have the same food products in two different areas of your kitchen, the bottom line is that these foods need to be in the stations where you are going to use them.

One of the other things that I like to remember when it comes to the Oatmeal Station is that there are a lot of fresh fruits that go great with the breakfast cereals. Apples, berries, bananas and peaches are just a few of the fabulous fruits that will compliment any breakfast.

OATMEAL STATION STAPLES

THESE ARE SOME OF THE BEST ITEMS TO START OUT YOUR OATMEAL STATION

Dry Grains: Steel Cut Oats, Old Fashioned Oats, Quick Oats, Cream of Wheat, Grits, Wheat Germ, Ground Flax Seed

Spice: Cinnamon, Allspice, Nutmeg, Apple Pie Spice, Pumpkin Pie Spice

Nuts: Pecans, Sliced Almonds, Walnuts

Dried Fruit: Raisins, Craisins, Dates, Prunes, Figs, Cherries, Blueberries

Sweeteners: Agave Nectar, Honey, Maple Syrup, Brown Sugar, Natural Sugar, Stevia

salad station

Salads are one of the best and easiest meals that we could ever have. I have salads almost every day and you should too. I actually have a full blown salad station in my refrigerator. Where most homes are loaded with meats, dairy, and cheese, mine is loaded with vegetables, fruits and everything you could possibly need to make great salads anytime.

It is a real simplicity to create fabulous salads, and create them fast. And in today's lifestyle of rush, rush, it is the ultimate solution to both health and convenience. One of the biggest obstacles to going vegan is that people say they just don't know how to cook anything vegan. Well, here is the easiest start to any vegan lifestyle, fresh salads! When your fridge is filled with the foods to make great salads, it's easy to produce quick easy meals anytime.

For the Salad Station, I claim the bottom half of the refrigerator and it is transformed into a great salad bar. I generally take the bottom two bins for the leafy greens and vegetables. One shelf up from there I have a huge air tight container that will hold enough precut leafy green mixes to last 3 to 4 days. I also have about 6 to 8 other containers on that same shelf that contain my cleaned and prepared vegetables of every kind.

One shelf up from there is where I would put my prepared salads like pasta salads, coleslaw, etc. That is also the shelf that I generally put my canned goods. I often keep canned goods that I am going to use for salads right in the refrigerator and that way they're already cold. If there are leftovers from canned goods, I put them right there too. Generally the upper shelf is for soy milk and juice, and I keep the top shelf just for leftovers, and prepped items to be cooked.

Once you get your refrigerator organized in this fashion, it is very easy to manage. Remember to keep everything rotated and also keep in mind to use variety. Having different meals will help keep the spoilage rates down. The really nice part about going vegan is that the

veggie foods in your refrigerator do not spoil anywhere near as fast as the meats and dairy, plus vegetables don't have the high contamination risk factor like meats.

Along with the Salad Station that is in the refrigerator, I have added a couple other staples that you want to always have on hand to make great salads. When you keep a strong Salad Station, you will be eating a lot healthier. I also find it quite refreshing to know that anytime a guest would show up, I can always whip up a fresh wholesome salad. My salad usage is daily, so I always have plenty for an unexpected guest.

You can run this concept into other stations. I like to have a little station just for the onions and potatoes that I use. The fresh fruit station filled with apples, oranges, and bananas should be visible for all to enjoy at any time. Then there is the canned food station, and you might even have a liquid station filled with oils, vinegars, sauces and any other condiments that have not yet made it to the fridge. A bakery station is also a great addition for the ones that love to bake.

Keep these stations organized and not too cluttered. Do proper rotations every single time you bring groceries home, I recommend using a marker and dating products. At least once every six months go through the shelves and set aside anything that has not been consumed in a while, to be used first. This way you will always have a kitchen that is filled with the fresh products that you need.

This process will not only keep you eating healthier, it will save you money. When you have everything you need at home to make quick and enjoyable meals, there is no need to dine out so often. This saves you a lot of money not just on the food itself, but the gas to run around, and time is money too. Quicker meals at home can actually be quicker than driving somewhere, standing in line, waiting for someone to cook it, and then driving back home. So turn your kitchen into the fun station that will be a great addition to your home life.

salad station

SALAD STATION STAPLES

THESE ARE JUST A FEW OF THE STAPLE PRODUCTS THAT I CARRY IN MY SALAD STATION.

REFRIGERATOR:

Leafy Greens: Romaine, Leaf Lettuce - red & green, Spinach, Kale, Endive, Cabbage

Vegetables: Broccoli, Carrots, Tomatoes, Onions - green, red and white, Peppers, Mushrooms, Cucumbers, Radishes, Celery

Fruits: Kiwi, Pears, Plums, Apples, Peaches, Pineapple

Citrus Fruits: Oranges, Lemons, Limes, Grapefruit

Herbs, Roots, & Flavor: Cilantro, Parsley, Basil, Mint, Garlic, Fire Roasted Red Bell Pepper, Ginger Root

Cooked Potatoes: I always have to have cooked potatoes of any kind because they make it so much easier to whip up a quick potato salad and can also be used for soups or even breakfast potatoes.

Frozen: Peas & Snow Peas, Asparagus, Brussels Sprouts, Beans of every kind - green, string, Italian, Corn

Note: These frozen foods work great in salads, run some cold water over them for a quick thaw and they're good to go. The freezing is also a form of cooking, as you are breaking down the fibers without losing a lot of nutrients like cooking does.

Dry Storage Goods: Canned Beans - Black, Kidney, Garbanzo, Pinto, Chow Mein Noodles, Croutons, Sunflower Seeds, Nuts

Dried Fruits: Raisins, Craisins, Dried Figs, Dried Apricots

Spices: Blackening Seasoning, Cajun Spice, Jamaican Jerk Rub, Chinese 5 Spice, Salt Free Seasonings, Lemon Zest, Orange Zest

Dressings & Condiments: Italian, Balsamic Vinegar, Raspberry Vinaigrette, Honey Mustard, Poppy Seed, Asian Toasted Sesame, Western Catalina, Dijon Mustard, and of course Olive Oil

Flavors: Mandarin Oranges, Pineapple, Peaches, Beets, Artichokes, Hearts of Palm, Salsa, Pickle Relish, Low Sodium Soy Sauce, Raspberry Preserves, Apricot Preserves, Orange Marmalade

beans, rice & pasta station

The next station that you will want to set up is the Beans Rice & Pasta Station. It is a simple station to set up, and it will be an easy one to maintain. Beans, rice and pastas are some of the greatest foundations to any vegan home.

When it comes to dried beans, there are many different types of beans. And there are even more combinations of beans like 15 bean soup bags that are easy to make. Try them all! One of my favorite things to do is the crock-pot bean soups because it's so easy to fill up the crock-pot with some beans, flavor and veggies, plug it in and it's done. It's a fun way to experiment too, and if the flavor is a little weak, you can always kick it up a notch at the end if you need to.

Rice is great too, and there are so many things you can do with it. One of my favorites is the parboiled rice because it holds its body quite well. When cooking rice, keep in mind that flavor comes from the outside, in. You can coat the rice with flavor, or you can cook the flavor into the rice. The other key element to rice cooking is the textures. By controlling the amount of water and cooking time, you can decide between firm and softer body. Types of rice can also contribute to the texture you're looking for.

Pastas are really fun to work with. The myth that you should put oil in the pasta is not necessary, you're wasting the oil, and it does absolutely nothing for the pasta. The reason people put a little salt into the boiling pot is because it will increase the boiling temperature of the water by 20+ degrees, thus preventing the pasta from sticking together. Pasta should be stirred often until it starts to boil. When you rinse it, use hot or warm water to rinse off excess starch from the pasta. If you are going to use the pasta later for salads or cooking, try a very small amount of oil to keep the pasta from sticking and then allow to air dry for a while to dry up the pasta. This will enable the pasta to absorb the flavors of the sauces you are mixing into it.

Just remember that beans, rice and pastas get old, and normally within a couple of years they will go bad. Beans will get so old that they will not soften when boiled. Rice can get stale and develop a rancid taste. And pastas will get to the point that they will fall apart into a mush when boiled.

HERE ARE SOME OF MY FAVORITE ITEMS TO FILL YOUR BEANS, RICE, & PASTA STATION

Dry Beans: Great Northern, Pinto, Kidney, Black, Split Peas, Small White, Lentils

Rice: Brown Rice, White Rice, Wild Rice, Parboiled Rice, Jasmine Rice

Pastas: Spaghetti, Fettuccine, Penne Pasta, Tricolor Spirals, Shells, Macaroni, Orzo, Bow Tie, Ziti

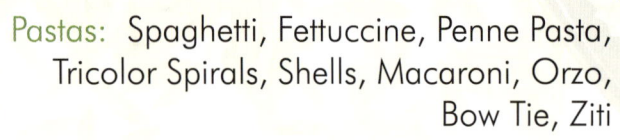

spice station

This is where the flavor hits the food. There is no better way to enhance the great foods God has provided than to have a well stocked Spice Station. Many of God's great foods are great just the way they are and I often eat the whole natural foods with no spices or seasonings whatsoever. It does take a little time for your taste buds to adjust to eating foods without the spices and salt, but in no time at all, you will grow to enjoy them. Most spices do have many health benefits, so don't be afraid to use them in abundance. It's a little bit of trial and error between your taste buds not needing all the spices when you go vegan and you developing a better tasting ability to really use more spices. When you do get all that fat and cholesterol off your taste buds, then you will really be able to taste all the great flavors that God has gifted us with in His herbs and spices.

I do tend to use the spices rather than the salt and pepper. You will get far better flavors this way and will be reducing your salt intake at the same time. There is also another factor that many of the spices have extremely strong health characteristics where as the salts and peppers do not.

Here are the best simplicity suggestions to bring flavor to your kitchen. You really don't need a lot of items to bring the flavor and there are certainly hundreds of other spices that are great, but here is a simple foundation to start with.

SPICES

Allspice: The flavor of ground allspice resembles a combination of pepper, clove, cinnamon, and nutmeg. It is used in many different dishes ranging from baking breads, pies and pastries. It is also great in soups, sauces, and entrees.

Cinnamon: Cinnamon has an exotic, sugary aroma and a sweet taste. It is used to enhance the flavors of sweet and savory dishes. It is used ground for the rich flavor you want in cakes, buns, pies, and cookies. Try in barbecue sauces for a fresh, light accent!

Cloves: Cloves can give great aromatic depth and flavor. They should have a high oil content which can sometimes causes plastic containers to haze slightly. Use in or on baked dishes, stews, chocolate puddings, vegetables, broiled grapefruit. Most often used in desserts, bread pudding, cookies, spice cake, and pumpkin pie.

Cumin: Ground cumin seeds have tremendous aroma and flavor. Cumin is most commonly used in chili powder, Indian curries, and Middle Eastern foods. It has a warm, earthy flavor. It can be purchased in ground or seed form. Whole seeds will stay fresh longer than ground.

Garlic: Garlic is widely used around the world for its pungent flavor as a seasoning or condiment. Garlic powder has a different taste from fresh garlic. If used as a substitute for fresh garlic, 1/8 teaspoon of garlic powder is equivalent to one clove of garlic.

Ginger: Ginger is known for its knobby root and a hot, peppery, and slightly sweet flavor. The most expensive and highest quality varieties generally come from Australia, South India, and Jamaica. It is associated with Asian and Indian cooking. Eastern cooking usually uses fresh ginger root grated, ground, and slivered in savory dishes. Europeans and Americans traditionally use the dried ground form. Ground ginger is used in gingerbread, cookies, pies, as well as in Indian curries, and Asian foods. Ginger is slightly hot, rich, and aromatic.

Mustard, Ground: There are literally dozens of different types of mustard both prepared and dry which come from a variety of mustard seeds. Its flavors are wide ranging and often used in every culture. Certainly one of the most widely used spices on the planet. The pungency of mustard is always reduced when heating. If added to a dish during cooking much of the flavor of the mustard is lost.

spice station

Nutmeg, Ground: Nutmeg is the actual seed of the tree, and in reality is a fruit. Nutmeg and mace have similar sensory qualities, nutmeg being slightly sweeter. Nutmeg is used for flavoring many dishes, from entrees to desserts.

Onion, dry: Onions are of course one of the main flavors and in the dry form, they can add surrounding flavor beyond the fresh chopped. Onion powder comes in a few varieties: white, yellow, red and toasted.

Paprika: Paprika is a spice made from the grinding of dried fruits, bell peppers or chili powders. In many languages, the word paprika refers to bell peppers themselves. The seasoning is used in many cuisines to add color and flavor to dishes. Paprika can range from mild to hot. Flavors also vary from country to country.

Turmeric, Ground: Turmeric grows wild in the forests of South and Southeast Asia and is a key ingredient for many Indian, Asian, and Persian dishes such as in curry and many more. It creates a unique flavor as well as color, especially popular for vegan dishes and tofu eggs.

Nutritional Yeast Flakes: Nutritional yeast is a deactivated yeast. It is popular with vegan dishes because of it is a source of protein and vitamins, especially the fortified B-12 vitamin. Nutritional yeast has a strong flavor that is described as nutty and cheesy, which makes it popular as an ingredient in cheese substitutes. Another popular use is as a topping for popcorn. It can also be used in mashed and fried potatoes, as well as put into scrambled tofu eggs.

BLENDS

Apple Pie Spice - Great for oatmeal

Pumpkin Pie Spice - Great for oatmeal

BBQ Spice - Great anytime

Curry powder - Great vegan dishes

Cajun Seasoning - Great anytime

Chicken Seasoning - Not for chicken, try it for soups and salads

Steak Seasoning - Not For steak, great on potatoes and tofu

Italian Seasoning - Great anytime

HERBS

Basil: Basil is great for tomatoes and sauces. It is also great for soups, stews, vegetables, and even tofu eggs.

Dill Weed: Dill weed has a great aromatic quality and can be used in both sauces and entrees. The flavor of many of your salads can be enhanced by adding dill.

Oregano: Also a great tomato addition. Oregano is popular in both Mexican and Italian cooking.

Bay Leaves: Bay leaves are often grown in Turkey. Green to pale green in color, they produce an aroma and flavor that is good for pickling, sauces, gravies, stews and soups.

spice station

Rosemary: These green leaves in the shape of pine needles are delectable in potatoes, stews, and vegetables. It is also powerful in BBQ smoking tofu.

Sage: This is a must have herb for stuffing, it can also be used in soups and stews.

Tarragon: I really like the licorice flavor that tarragon produces. Not only is it great in salads and entries but also try it on some cooked carrots.

Thyme: Thyme gives pleasing flavor to soups, breads, stews, stuffing, casseroles, and compound butters. Thyme is aromatic, with a warm, pungent flavor. It has been popular for centuries; from ancient Greeks to the present, and in most all types of cuisines.

EXTRACTS

Vanilla: A must have for every spice station. Look for the alcohol free.

Almond: A must have for every spice station.

SALT & PEPPERS

Celery Salt: This salt can really help you get flavor into your salads, soups, stews and even vegetables.

Hickory Smoked Salt: Hickory salt is great for breads, tofu on the BBQ,
and many entrees or sides where you are looking for that natural smoke element.

Red Chili Peppers Flakes: These little flakes can give a nice popping action of pepper to any dish. Just be careful not to over do it. The longer they are in contact with liquid, the hotter they will get.

Lemon Pepper: Always tasty on a salad, and if you don't use pepper, there are great lemon zests too.

Red Pepper: The best way to get some warmth to any dish is the red or cayenne pepper.

Chili Powder: There are dozens of chili powders and each one can present a unique flavor to your cooking creations.

EXTRAS

Lemon Juice: A must have for every home.

Soy Sauce: A must have. There is also low sodium soy sauce or Braggs liquid aminos which are very good sources of flavor.

Spices give you flavor, but just don't over do it, especially when it comes to the salt and pepper. For more great spice information, flavors, and how to use them, you can go to my website at www.chefmarkanthony.com

breakfast
simplicity

breakfast simplicity

The simplicity of breakfast is something you will savor even more than the smell of maple syrup and steaming fresh pancakes right off the griddle. The ease of morning meals really does make it a blessing to have your biggest meal in the morning. Waffles and tofu eggs, healthy vegan muffins, breakfast burritos, and biscuits with gravy are just a fraction of the great tasting meals you can be indulging into every day.

I do love my oatmeal and am a consistent consumer of oatmeal creations. I could do a different oatmeal every day of the year. Very often I will accompany my oatmeal with a bagel and vegan cream cheese or maybe some whole wheat toast. The morning is when I do my biggest consumption of carbs. Eat all you want, stuff yourself like a king. The calories that you consume in the morning will all be burned off before the day is half over.

Beyond the simplicity of actually preparing meals for breakfast, I do like some of the ready-made elements that God has supplied us with. Fruit is something I can eat anytime, but I don't think I ever go a day without a banana or two, especially for breakfast. Bananas are one of the healthiest fruits we could ever eat and they are generally one of the lowest priced fruits on the market. Very often I will blanket my oatmeal with bananas, berries, or a whole chopped apple. I also enjoy the dried fruits as a morning treat.

Nuts are another great way to start the day. We can get a lot of the protein, fiber and essential oils just by having a few nuts. A couple almonds, pecans, and walnuts will round off any morning with joy.

Juice and soy milk are always a welcome addition to any breakfast, but I do not recommend the processed store bought items. They are generally loaded with sugars and chemicals. If you are going to get the store bought, at least look at the labels and find the products without all the sugar. Try to stick with making your own, juicers are great! But if you are going to get the store bought, at least look at the labels and find the ones without all the sugar.

Start every day with a great breakfast. It will help you lose weight, give you more energy throughout the day, and keep you living a healthier, happier, and a longer, more vibrant life.

breakfast simplicity

Raspberry Banana Tofu Muffins

INGREDIENTS:

1 cup silken tofu

2/3 cup maple syrup

1/4 cup flax seed oil

1 Tbsp vanilla extract

1 large banana, ripe

2 cups unbleached flour

1/2 cup whole wheat flour

1 1/2 tsp baking soda

1 1/2 tsp baking powder

1/4 tsp sea salt

1 1/2 cup raspberries

DIRECTIONS:

Preheat oven to 350 degrees. Process tofu, syrup, oil, vanilla and banana in a food processor until smooth.
In a separate bowl, sift together flours, baking soda, baking powder and salt. Pour tofu mixture into the flour mixture and gently whisk together. Gently fold in raspberries. Line a muffin pan with 12 unbleached muffin cups. Fill each cup about 3/4 full with batter. Bake for about 20 minutes, or until golden.

breakfast simplicity

Veg-Confetti Muffins

INGREDIENTS:

1 cup whole wheat pastry flour

1 cup unbleached white flour

1/4 cup ground flax seed

2 Tbsp baking powder

1 Tbsp cinnamon

1/2 tsp salt

1/2 cup apple sauce

1/3 cup agave nectar

3 Tbsp maple syrup

1 cup grated carrot

1 cup grated zucchini

1 cup diced apple

1 cup chopped walnuts

DIRECTIONS:

Preheat oven to 375 degrees. Mix dry ingredients of flour, flax seed, baking powder, cinnamon, and salt. In another bowl, mix agave nectar, maple syrup & applesauce. Pulse zucchini, carrot, apple and walnut in food processor until finely chopped. Add dry mixture to the wet ingredients and stir well. Place into muffin tins around 2/3 full and bake for about 25 minutes, until golden. Makes about 15 muffins.

breakfast simplicity

Low-Fat Blueberry Muffins

INGREDIENTS:

4 cups flour

2 Tbsp baking powder

1 tsp salt

1 tsp cinnamon

1 1/2 cups natural sugar

Egg replacer equivalent to 4 eggs

4 Tbsp water

1 tsp vanilla

1 1/2 cup soy milk — or rice milk

1 1/2 cup applesauce

1 1/2 cup blueberries — fresh or frozen (measured then defrosted)

DIRECTIONS:

Preheat the oven to 400 degrees. Mix the first 5 dry ingredients together, and then add all the wet ones. Mix just until moistened, and not over mixing. Fold in the blueberries and then fill muffin cups full. Bake 20 minutes until browned and cooked through. Makes about 2 dozen muffins.

breakfast simplicity

Applesauce Muffins

INGREDIENTS:

1 cup whole wheat flour

1 cup unbleached white flour

1 Tbsp baking powder

1/2 tsp salt

1 tsp cinnamon

1/3 cup sugar

1/2 tsp stevia powder

Egg replacer for 2 large eggs

1/2 cup soy milk

1 cup applesauce

1/2 cup raisins, optional

DIRECTIONS:

Preheat the oven to 375 degrees. Mix the first 5 dry ingredients together, and mix all the wet ones with the sweeteners. Combine the 2 mixtures together and fill paper lined muffin tins full. Bake about 20 to 25 minutes until golden.

breakfast simplicity

Banana Date Nut Muffins

INGREDIENTS:

2 cups whole wheat flour

1 1/2 cups unbleached white flour

2 Tbsp baking powder

3/4 tsp salt

1 Tbsp cinnamon

1 cup natural sugar

7 very ripe bananas, mashed

1 cup vanilla soy milk

1 cup natural apple sauce

1/2 cup chopped dates

1/2 cup chopped walnuts

DIRECTIONS:

Preheat the oven to 400 degrees. Sift together the flours, baking powder, salt, and cinnamon. In another bowl, mash the banana with the sugar, soy milk, and apple sauce.
Pour the banana mixture into the flour mixture and stir just until combined. Add in the dates and walnuts, and pour into muffin cups. Bake for 15-20 minutes, until a toothpick comes out clean. Makes about 2 dozen muffins

No Fat Drop Biscuits

INGREDIENTS:

1 cup unbleached white flour

1 cup whole wheat pastry flour

1/2 tsp baking soda

1/2 tsp salt

1 tsp sugar

1 tsp baking powder

1 1/4 cups reduced-fat soy milk mixed with

1 Tbsp Lemon juice

DIRECTIONS:

Preheat oven to 400 degrees. Mix the dry ingredients together in a medium bowl. Stir in soy milk with a fork. Stir quickly to moisten the dry ingredients. Drop the mixture by large spoonfuls onto lightly greased or non-stick cookie sheets. Bake at 400 degrees for about 10 minutes, or until golden brown on the bottom and beginning to color on the top.

VARIATION:

For herbal biscuits, add a few of the following: 1/4 tsp pepper, 1/2 tsp minced garlic, 1 Tbsp minced fresh basil, 2 Tbsp minced fresh chives, and 1 tsp minced fresh oregano, thyme, and marjoram to the dry mixture.

breakfast simplicity

Vegan Country Gravy

INGREDIENTS:

6 Tbsp olive oil

1/2 cup Unbleached Flour

1 quart Soy Milk

4 vegan breakfast sausage patties

Pinch sea salt to taste

Pinch of crushed red pepper flakes, if you like it spicy

1 tsp red pepper

DIRECTIONS:

In a large heavy bottomed sauce pan, sauté your favorite vegan sausage until brown and then crumble into small pieces. Remove the sausage from the pan and set aside. Add the oil and stir in the flour to make a roux. Cook this oil and flour mixture over low heat until the flour is a creamy brown, stirring often with a whisk to prevent burning. Roux takes on a creamy brown color when cooked.

Preheat the plain soy milk over medium heat until hot, but not boiling.

Pour half of the soy milk into the bubbling browned flour and whisk quickly. Then add the remainder and whisk until smooth. Add the crumbled sausage pieces and stir into the gravy.

Remember that the gravy will solidify as it cools. If you reheat the cold gravy leftovers after refrigeration, you may have to add a little soy milk to get it back to a serving consistency.

breakfast simplicity

Crepes

INGREDIENTS:

1/2 cup soy milk

1/2 cup water

1/4 cup melted soy margarine

1 Tbsp natural sugar

2 Tbsp maple syrup

1 cup unbleached all-purpose flour

1/4 tsp salt

DIRECTIONS:

In a large mixing bowl, blend soy milk, water, 1/4 cup margarine, sugar, syrup, flour, and salt. Cover and chill the mixture for 2 hours.

Lightly grease a 6 inch skillet with some soy margarine. Heat the skillet until hot. Pour approximately 4 tablespoons of batter into the skillet. Swirl to make the batter cover the skillet's bottom. Cook until golden, flip and cook on opposite side.

These crepes are now ready to stuff with your favorite flavors. You can serve or hold in oven at 150 degrees.

Basic Tofu Eggs

INGREDIENTS:

1 block extra firm tofu, drained

2 Tbsp oil or margarine

1 tsp garlic powder

1 tsp onion powder

2 Tbsp nutritional yeast

1 tsp chicken style seasoning

1/2 tsp turmeric

DIRECTIONS:

Crumble the tofu into desired size pieces and cook in oil for 3-5 minutes, stirring often. Add remaining ingredients, reduce heat to medium and allow to cook 5-10 more minutes, stirring frequently and adding more oil if needed. Some people like the browning action that the tofu eggs will take if you leave them setting in the pan without stirring.

These eggless eggs are ready for a handful of different applications including burritos, casseroles and sandwiches.

ADD ONS: I would recommend sauteing diced onions and peppers into the mixture for a far greater flavor. Another great flavor add on is lime zest, jerk rub, chopped cilantro, and allspice, giving it a Jamaican flavor twist.

oatmeal simplicity

As you have noticed in the Oatmeal Station section, it is extremely easy to have great meals every morning when you have the right products on hand. It is one of the fastest, easiest, and healthiest meals you can ever produce.

One of the tricks that I do when I am on the road is to use my coffee pot for making hot water. I will take a bowl and fill it 3/4 full of quick oats, fill it with water, give it a quick stirring, and then let it set for 5 minutes, and it's ready to enjoy. No microwaving, no cooking water on the stove, just fast and easy on the road. Then I take it and top it with everything you could possibly think of. Here are some great oatmeal suggestions.

It doesn't matter if you have rolled oats, or steel-cut oats, quick oats, or whole oats; they're all great for you and can all be flavored in countless ways. I also include cream of wheat and grits in the simplicity of oatmeal. They too can be flavored many ways. There is also millet, which makes for a great breakfast treat, especially when it is topped with cherry or blueberry filling.

Try some of these great ways to keep variety in your breakfast. Starting out with a great breakfast is the best habit you can do for a healthier you.

Slow Cooker Banana Pudding Oatmeal

INGREDIENTS:

1 cup steel-cut oats

4 cups Almond milk

1 Tbsp vanilla extract

2 bananas, mashed

3 Tbsp agave nectar

DIRECTIONS:

The night before: Spray your crock-pot with oil. Add oats, almond milk, and vanilla. Cook on low over night, about 8 hours.

In the morning: Stir your oatmeal well. It may appear watery on the top but if stirred it should become a more uniform consistency. Stir in sweetener, mashed bananas and it's ready to eat. You can add additional banana slices and even some vanilla wafers on the top for an extra wow factor.

oatmeal simplicity

Crock-Pot Almond Joy Oatmeal

INGREDIENTS:

1 cup steel-cut oats

4 cups unsweetened coconut milk

4 tablespoons finely shredded unsweetened coconut

2 tsp vanilla extract

1 tsp almond extract

4 Tbsp agave nectar

DIRECTIONS:

The night before: Spray your crock-pot with some oil. Add all ingredients, except sweetener, and cook on low over night for about 8 hours.

In the morning: Stir your oatmeal well. It may appear watery on the top but if stirred it should become a more uniform consistency. Stir in sweetener and top each serving with some slivered almonds.

oatmeal simplicity

Slow Cooker Lemon Blueberry Oatmeal

INGREDIENTS:

1 cup steel-cut oats

4 cups unsweetened coconut milk

2 cups blueberries

1 Tbsp vanilla extract

1 tsp lemon extract

4 Tbsp agave nectar

DIRECTIONS:

The night before: Spray your crock-pot with some oil. Add everything except sweetener and cook on low over night for about 8 hours.

In the morning: Stir your oatmeal well. It may appear watery on the top but if stirred it should become a more uniform consistency. Smash in any floating blueberries and stir in sweetener. Garnish with some fresh blueberries and sprinkle with fresh lemon zest.

This oatmeal reminds me of my favorite muffin. You get blueberries in every bite with a bright burst of lemon. There's something about just smelling lemon that seems to make the yuckiest day seem to have possibilities.

oatmeal simplicity

Crock-Pot Grain Delight

INGREDIENTS:

1 cup hard red wheat

1 cup brown rice

5 cups water

1/4 tsp sea salt

DIRECTIONS:

Spraying the crock with oil helps the clean up. Put all ingredients in a crockpot on low overnight and it's ready.

Top with your favorite toppings; honey, soy milk, fruit, nuts, etc.

[*If God made it, eat it*

and if Man made it, Don't.

Jack LaLanne]

Quinoa Hot Breakfast Cereal

INGREDIENTS:

1 cup quinoa

2 cups water

1 Tbsp natural sugar

1 fine chopped apple

1/3 cup raisins

1/2 teaspoon cinnamon

DIRECTIONS:

Rinse the quinoa in water using a strainer. Add the quinoa to the water in a medium sized saucepan. Bring to a boil, reduce heat and simmer for 5 minutes. Add the apples, raisins and cinnamon. Simmer until the water has been absorbed. Serve with milk of your choice and sweeten with honey or syrup if desired.

granola
simplicity

granola simplicity

Granola is simply defined as a combination of rolled oats, nuts and honey. Over the years it has reinvented itself into many combinations including rice, dried fruits, such as raisins and dates, ground flax seed, and coconut. Baked granola is the most popular, but there is a "muesli" style, which is a no-cooked type of granola. Granola is great for breakfast, snacks and even desserts and parfaits.

There is also the invention of the granola bars that have maintained the reputation of being a healthy snack even though the majority of them are actually loaded with sugar and salt. So be careful of the granolas, or even better, make your own. It's extremely easy to make granolas, you will save a lot of money, and it will be a lot healthier for you than the sugar powered, chemical laced granolas that we find in the grocery stores.

GENERAL GRANOLA RECIPE GUIDELINES

The basic process is to take a combination of dry products, mix #1, and mix them with a wet combination, mix #2. Then we need to spread thin the combined ingredients on sheet pans and place in a 250 degree oven for about 1 to 1 1/2 hours, stirring about every 15 minutes until golden brown. Then place in a bowl and mix with the #3 mix ingredients. And that easy, you have granola.

Note: A secret to making chunky granolas is to press it together with your fist, making clumps. Then try not to stir the clumps until they have baked together.

Basic Granola Recipe

MIX #1

3 cups rolled oats
1 cup slivered almonds
3/4 cup shredded coconut

MIX #2

1/3 cup dark brown sugar
1/3 cup maple syrup
1/4 cup vegetable oil
3/4 tsp salt

MIX #3

1/2 cup raisins
1/2 cup craisins

It's really that easy. Try many different combinations. You really can't go wrong. One of the things I like to do is make big batches and keep them in my oatmeal station. I put them in airtight jars, label the front, and have them for breakfast cereal with fresh sliced bananas or fruits of any field.

It's also nice to place snack size amounts in little plastic baggies for snacks and on the go times. Whatever way you make them, they're great. So dive into one of the easiest vegan dishes you could ever make.

granola simplicity

Pumpkin Granola

MIX #1

14 cups rolled oats

MIX #2

1 16oz can pumpkin

1 can coconut milk

1 cup maple syrup

1 cup brown sugar

MIX #3

1 cup fine chopped walnuts

2 cups craisins

2 cups coconut chips

Low Fat / Sugar Granola

Here is granola recipe with no added fat.

MIX #1

3 cups rolled oats

1/2 cup wheat or oat bran

1/2 cup wheat germ

1/2 cup coarsely chopped almonds

1/4 cup raw sunflower seeds

MIX #2

1 Tbsp ground cinnamon

1/4 cup maple syrup

MIX #3

1 cup raisins

1/2 cup coarsely chopped, pitted dates

granola simplicity

Almond Maple Granola

MIX #1

3 cups rolled oats

1 cup blanched slivered almonds

1/4 cup wheat germ

2 cups flaked coconut

1/3 cup unsalted sunflower seeds (optional)

MIX #2

1/3 cup pure maple syrup

1/3 cup packed dark brown sugar

1/4 cup vegetable oil

2 Tbsp warm water

1/2 tsp salt

MIX #3

1 cup raisins

Chunky Date Granola

MIX #1

3 cups old-fashioned oats

1 cup whole almonds, halved

1/2 cup coconut, large chips

1/2 cup raw cashews

1/2 cup brown sugar

1 Tbsp ground allspice

1 tsp ground cinnamon

MIX #2

1/4 cup vegan margarine, melted

1/4 cup honey

MIX #3

1 1/2 cup (packed) pitted dates, cut crosswise into thirds

gourmet bar
simplicity

gourmet bar simplicity

Bars are really easy to make and there are a number of different ways they can created. There are the dry crunchy bars which is generally a baked bar and some people even do a form of dehydrating to give it that raw food staple.

Another bar which is one of my favorites is the no cook bars. One of the easiest ways to do these is again a mix #1, mix #2, and mix #3 process.

Mix #1 is a combination of dried fruits that are blended in a food processor until they form a ball. Depending on the moisture in the fruit, it may take a little time, I like the mixture well formed.

Mix #2 is your dried items. This can consist of many foods; nuts of every kind like cashews, almonds, walnuts. Seeds like flax, sunflower, and pumpkin are great too. You can also use many great compliments like oatmeal, coconut, and spices like cinnamon or allspice. This mixture #2 can be left whole, or ground into an extra fine chopped, depending on your preferred creation. I sometimes reserve a bit of the combination for a whole nut and fine chop the rest. We will then combine mixtures #1 and #2 and continue pulsing to incorporate the two mixtures together. The greater amount of mixture #2, the drier the final product will be. This combination of mixtures can now be placed into a bowl and then add mixture #3.

Mix #3 is the sweeteners, oil and salt. It doesn't take a lot and is often really not a necessary step, but you will find that it does add flavor to a lot of the recipes. And the little bit of optional oil does help aid in the product not sticking to everything it touches nearly as much.

You will want to knead the final product for about 5 minutes. And then press into a cookie sheet that is covered with saran wrap. An easy way to do this is to place another sheet of saran wrap on the top and use a rolling pin to press bars into the desired thickness. Cut into desired shapes, even freezing or refrigerating for a while will help get a better cut if your mixture is too soft.

These bars can be frosted different ways, or maybe you want to roll them into balls and sprinkle them with nuts or toppings. You can wrap them and they are good to go on the go. So have fun and play around with the simplicity of bar making.

Ultimate Gourmet Bars

MIX #1

1/2 cup dried cherries

1/2 cup dried cranberries

1/2 cup dried dates

1/2 cup dried figs

1/2 cup golden raisins

MIX #2 (everything is optional)

1/2 cup raw sunflower seeds

1 cup raw almond slices

1 cup raw cashews

1/4 cup raw pecans

1/4 cup raw pumpkin seeds

1/2 cup ground flax seed

1 cup unsweetened dried coconut

1/2 cup dehydrated bananas

1/2 cup oatmeal (optional, regular or toasted)

MIX #3 (everything is optional but recommended)

1 tsp ground cinnamon

1/2 tsp salt (optional)

5 Tbsp brown rice syrup, agave syrup, honey or maple syrup

1/4 cup rice bran oil or safflower oil

gourmet bar simplicity

Oatmeal Breakfast Bars

INGREDIENTS:

3 cups rolled oats

1/2 cup soy protein powder

1/4 cup natural sugar

2 tsp baking powder

1 tsp cinnamon

1/4 tsp salt

1/2 cup applesauce

1 Tbsp honey

1 tsp vanilla

Egg Replacer equaling 2 eggs

1 cup soy milk

1/3 cup raisins

1/3 cup dried cranberries

DIRECTIONS:

Preheat oven to 350 degrees.

Mix the dry ingredients together in a large bowl. Mix the wet ingredients together in another bowl. Combine the wet and dry ingredients and mix together. Mix in raisins and cranberries. Press into a 13 x 9 inch nonstick pan lightly coated with oil. Bake 25 to 35 minutes. Cut into rectangular shaped bars.

Fig Bars

FILLING INGREDIENTS:

8 oz. dried figs

4 oz. pitted dates

2 Tbsp almonds, slivered

2 drops anise extract

1 Tbsp agave nectar

2 Tbsp water

1 Tbsp lemon juice

1/4 tsp cinnamon

1/8 tsp ginger

CRUST INGREDIENTS

1 cup regular or quick oats, ground in blender until fine

1 cup regular or quick oats, not ground

1 tsp baking powder

1/4 tsp salt

1/4 cup unsweetened apple sauce

3 Tbsp agave nectar

1/4 cup water

DIRECTIONS:

Preheat oven to 375 degrees. For the filling, put the figs, dates, and almonds into the food processor. Grind to a coarse paste. Stir in the remaining filling ingredients and process until mixed. Set aside.

For the crust, combine the dry ingredients in a mixing bowl. Stir in the wet ingredients, mixing well to a thick consistency. Press half the crust mixture into the bottom of a lightly oiled, eight-inch square cake pan. Spread the fig mixture evenly over the crust. Smooth the remaining crust mixture over the filling. Bake for about 30 minutes, until lightly browned. Allow to cool completely before cutting.

ICING OPTION:

Mix about 1/4 cup of powdered sugar with a little water, 1 teaspoon at a time until you get the desired consistency. A few drops of vanilla, almond or lemon extract will really enhance the taste. Drizzle over top of bars. Makes 16 bars.

pancake & waffle
simplicity

pancake & waffle simplicity

Pancakes are one of the easiest meals to produce and they're not just for breakfast. Far too often we place food into these time boxes and don't realize that good food is good food regardless of when you eat it. I do try to eat a lot more carbs in the morning because they carry me through the day and I will burn them off.

When making pancakes, keep in mind that, like most baking, it is a dry mix/wet mix process. I really do recommend mixing the product, waiting 5 minutes and then mixing again. This will give you the true consistency and eliminate excess lumps. If the mixture is too thick, add more water, too thin, add a little bit more flour.

Now an easy way to cheat is to just use a pre-made mix. Just read the labels and don't get the buttermilk ones. There are products like Bisquick that are all vegan and you can ignore the directions about the oil, milk and eggs, and just add water.

You can jazz up any pancake with the flavorings like cinnamon or vanilla. Adding fruit is easy too. You can mix fruit into the batter but just be careful because there is a higher sticking probability. I often pour the pancake on the grill and then drop the fruit on the cooking pancakes, then flip. Be careful to cook a little longer on the flip side to ensure that the batter is fully cooked.

Flavoring can also be poured on top as in the form of syrups, hot thickened fruits, and sprinklings of fresh fruits or nuts. Add a dollop of vegan whip cream! You can even make stuffed pancakes, stuff and roll them with fruit or vegan cream cheese. So get really creative with them. You could even have pancakes with beef-less stew, or pancake sandwiches. In all reality, it's just another form of bread.

Waffles can often use the same mixture as pancakes. You just need to be careful of the fruits and sugars that tend to stick to the waffle irons.

So, however you make your pancakes and waffles, they really are easy and you can even get the younger ones to help in the kitchen. Make it a family event.

Whole Wheat Vegan Pancakes

INGREDIENTS:

DRY:

1 1/2 cups whole wheat flour

3 Tbsp sugar

1 1/2 tsp baking powder

1/4 tsp salt

Mix the dry ingredients well and set aside.

WET:

1 1/2 cups soy milk

2 Tbsp ground flax seed mixed with 6 tbsp water

3 Tbsp oil

1 tsp vanilla

Mix the wet and then combine with the dry.

pancake & waffle simplicity

Simple Golden Pancakes

INGREDIENTS:

DRY:

1 cup flour

1 Tbsp sugar

1 Tbsp baking powder

1/8 tsp salt

Mix the dry ingredients well and set aside.

WET:

1 cup soy milk

2 Tbsp vegetable oil

Mix the wet and then combine with the dry.

Homemade Maple Syrup

INGREDIENTS:

2 cups white sugar

1 cup boiling water

1 Tbsp maple flavored extract

DIRECTIONS:

In a saucepan, combine sugar and water. Cook and stir until sugar is dissolved. Remove from heat, and stir in maple flavoring.
Serve warm.

Simple Whole Wheat Waffles

INGREDIENTS:

DRY: WET:

1 cup whole wheat flour   1 cup soy milk

3/4 tsp baking powder   2 Tbsp vegetable oil

3 Tbsp sugar   Mix the wet and then combine with the dry.

1/4 tsp cinnamon

Pinch of sea salt

Mix the dry ingredients well and set aside.

[Eat things that are a plant *and not the things* that were manufactured in a plant.

Mark Anthony]

Oatmeal Raisin Pancakes

DRY INGREDIENTS:

3 cups oatmeal

1 cup whole wheat flour

4 tsp baking powder

1 Tbsp cinnamon

Mix the dry ingredients well and then add:

2 1/2 cups low-fat soy milk

1/2 cup raisins

DIRECTIONS:

Make like regular pancakes by cooking in a lightly oiled pan and flipping when frequent bubbles appear. Makes about 15 pancakes.

Delicious Orange Pancakes

DRY INGREDIENTS:

1 1/4 cups unbleached white flour

1 cup whole wheat flour

1/4 cup reduced-fat soy milk powder

4 tsp baking powder

2 tsp baking soda

1 tsp salt

Mix the dry ingredients well and then add:

WET INGREDIENTS:

1 cup apple juice

2 cups orange juice

DIRECTIONS:

Make like regular pancakes by cooking in a lightly oiled pan and flipping when frequent bubbles appear. Makes about 15 pancakes.

beverages & blending
simplicity

beverages & blending simplicity

Blending is one of the greatest ways to get the nutrition that we all need. I will be bold enough to say that you can blend almost anything. Blending is a great way to expand your creativity, and it is always a pleasant welcome for any guest.

One of the things to keep in mind when it comes to blending is the types of juices you are purchasing. Many of the juices in the grocery stores are merely sugar water, and containing everything from high-fructose corn syrup to aspartame. These juices are often just as bad as the sugary sodas, in their contribution to obesity and diabetes. They are hiding their harmful poisons behind the deceptive labels of health that the word "juice" retains.

Even some of the juices labeled 100% fruit juice will still be from concentrate and nutrient weak because of the pasteurization process. Fresh fruit is best! Sometimes it takes a little getting used to and that's because you're not getting all the sugar, salt and chemicals, but in no time at all your taste buds will adapt to the healthier beverages, and the manufactured beverages will actually be an unappealing product, even having a disgusting flavor.

JUICE BLEND: Is a blend of juices with no ice and no whole fruit

SMOOTHIE: Is a pureed fruit drink. Often made with frozen fruits, bananas, or tofu.

SLUSH DRINK: Is an ice and fruit juice style, sometimes slang termed slurpie.

FRAPPÉ: A partially frozen, often fruity drink. Traditionally, it is usually a mixture of ingredients served over a mound of crushed ice.

PUNCH: A party-size beverage consisting of fruit, fruit juices, flavorings and some form of sweetener.

A MOCKTAIL OR VIRGIN: A non-alcoholic drink.

LACE: Applies to the last ingredient in a recipe, meaning to pour onto the top of the drink, often to get a layered visual effect.

beverages & blending simplicity

Blueberry Tofu Blend

INGREDIENTS:

3/4 cup frozen blueberries

1 ripe banana

1 cup vanilla soy milk

3 ounces silken tofu

DIRECTIONS:

Combine all ingredients for selected recipe in a blender. Puree until completely smooth. Serve immediately.

[He who has health has hope; and he who has hope has *everything.*
Arabian Proverb]

beverages & blending simplicity

Kiwi Honeydew Blend

INGREDIENTS:

2 cups honeydew, peeled, seeded & cubed

2 cups crushed ice

1 1/2 cups kiwi peeled and cut

10 large fresh mint leaves

1 Tbsp fresh lime juice

1 Tbsp honey

DIRECTIONS:

Combine all ingredients in blender and process until smooth.

Fresh Homemade Tomato Juice

INGREDIENTS:

3 pounds very ripe tomatoes, cored & chopped

1 1/4 cups chopped celery with leaves

1/3 cup chopped onion

2 Tbsp natural sugar

1 tsp sea salt or to taste

Pinch red pepper

Tabasco sauce, about 6-8 drops

DIRECTIONS:

Put all ingredients into a large non-reactive pot (stainless steel, not aluminum). Bring to a simmer and cook, uncovered, until mixture is completely soupy, about 30 minutes.

Force mixture through a sieve, food mill, or cheese cloth. Cool completely. Store covered and chilled. Makes about 1 quart.

NOTE: Depending on their ripeness and the variety of tomato, some tomatoes are sweeter than others. Use the ripest tomatoes you can find. Added sugar will balance the natural acidity of the tomatoes, use more or less to taste. Tabasco hot sauce is also to taste, depending on your desired level of spiciness.

salad
simplicity

salad simplicity

One of the easiest items to make are fresh salads and sometimes I can't even do a recipe for a salad because they are just too easy to make. So here are some great visions of salads that you can make anytime. Sometimes a picture is worth a thousand words.

Keep in mind that the salads themselves are extremely healthy, yet many people will ruin their efforts by loading them up with extreme amounts of salad dressings. Many of the dressings are loaded with high calories and fat. Beyond the fat and calories is the high fructose corn syrup and refined sugar that is often present, and that's not to mention the chemicals and additives. So make sure to read those labels and find the dressings that are healthier, or better yet, make your own.

Most of the dressings you would make for home use will have an extremely long shelf life, even into the weeks and months. Lemon or vinegar are good preservative agents. The other factor to consider when it comes to using dressings is to use less. I actually use about 1/2 the dressing than I did years ago. It is actually a preference to me now to have less. Once you get the flavor, you're there.

salad simplicity

Light Bean Salad

INGREDIENTS:

- 1 - 15 oz. can black beans, rinsed
- 1 - 15 oz. can kidney beans, rinsed
- 1 - 15 oz. can cannellini beans, rinsed
- 1 green bell pepper, chopped
- 1 red bell pepper, chopped
- 1 - 10 oz. package frozen corn kernels
- 1 red onion, chopped

Olive Oil Dressing

INGREDIENTS:

- 1/2 cup extra virgin olive oil
- 1/2 cup red wine vinegar
- 2 Tbsp fresh lime juice
- 1 Tbsp lemon juice
- 1/4 cup natural sugar
- 1 Tbsp sea salt
- 2 cloves crushed garlic
- 1/4 cup cilantro, fresh chopped
- 1/2 Tbsp ground cumin
- 1/2 Tbsp red pepper
- Optional heat: 2 dashes hot pepper sauce, 1 teaspoon chili powder

DIRECTIONS:

In a large bowl, combine beans, bell peppers, frozen corn, and red onion. In a small bowl, whisk together olive oil, red wine vinegar, lime juice, lemon juice, sugar, salt, garlic, cilantro, cumin, and red pepper. Season to taste with hot sauce and chili powder.

Pour dressing over vegetables and mix well. Chill thoroughly and serve cold.

salad simplicity

Asian Tofu Salad

INGREDIENTS:

3 Tbsp olive oil

2 Tbsp rice vinegar

1 Tbsp honey

1 Tbsp soy sauce, reduced-sodium

1 tsp sesame oil

1 tsp ginger, fresh minced

1/2 tsp sea salt

14 ounce tofu, extra-firm, drained and diced 1-inch cubes

8 cup mixed greens lettuce

2 medium carrots, peeled, and asian sliced

1 large cucumber, chopped

DIRECTIONS:

In a bowl, whisk olive oil with vinegar, honey, soy sauce, sesame oil, ginger and salt. Place tofu and 2 tablespoons of the dressing in a large nonstick skillet. Cook over medium-high heat, turning every 2 to 3 minutes, until golden brown, about 10 minutes. Remove from the heat, add 1 tablespoon of the dressing to the pan and stir, coat tofu with dressing.

Toss greens, carrots and cucumber with the remaining dressing. Top with the warm tofu and serve immediately.

salad simplicity

Thai Papaya Salad

INGREDIENTS:

1 small green papaya

1/2 cup honey-roasted peanuts

1 1/2 cups bean sprouts

1 medium tomato, cut into long thin strips

1 red chili, minced (seeds removed if you prefer a milder salad)

3 green onions, sliced into long matchstick-like pieces

1/2 cup fresh basil, roughly chopped

1/8 cup of fresh coriander

DRESSING:

3 Tbsp soy sauce

2 Tbsp olive oil

3 Tbsp lime juice

1 Tbsp honey

DIRECTIONS:

Prepare the dressing by mixing all the dressing ingredients together in a bowl. Set aside.

Peel the green papaya, then slice it in half and remove all the seeds. Using the largest grater you have, grate the papaya (or you can use a potato peeler to create thin, ribbon-like strips). Place in a large bowl.

Add the sliced tomato, green onion, chili, bean sprouts, and most of the basil. Add the dressing, tossing to combine. Add the peanuts and toss again.

To serve, scoop the salad into individual bowls or onto a serving platter. Sprinkle with remaining basil leaves plus fresh coriander. Serve immediately and ENJOY!

NOTE: your papaya should be very firm, the flesh white to light orange in color.

salad dressing
simplicity

salad dressing simplicity

Easy Italian Dressings

You can create this dry mixture of seasonings and store in an airtight container, then when you're ready to make dressing, it's ready to use.

INGREDIENTS:

- 2 Tbsp sea salt
- 2 Tbsp dried oregano
- 1 Tbsp dried parsley
- 1 Tbsp garlic salt
- 1 Tbsp onion powder
- 1 Tbsp natural sugar
- 1 tsp dried basil
- 1 tsp red pepper
- 1/2 tsp dried thyme
- 1/4 tsp celery salt

DIRECTIONS:

Mix all ingredients well.

TO PREPARE A DRESSING:

Whisk together

1/4 cup white vinegar or lemon juice

2/3 cup olive oil

2 Tbsp water

2 Tbsp of the dry Italian mixture.

NOTE: This dry mixture also does well with veganaise and cream cheese for vegan dips. You can also add a bit of soy milk for a great creamy Italian dressing.

Oil-Free Balsamic Vinaigrette

INGREDIENTS:

3/4 cup water

1/2 cup balsamic vinegar

1/4 cup lemon juice

1/4 tsp dry mustard

4 cloves garlic, minced

1 tsp salt

1/4 tsp Guar gum

DIRECTIONS:

Combine all ingredients in a blender, and blend on high speed until well combined and smooth. Transfer to a bottle or jar.

NOTE: Guar gum is a dried, ground powder that comes from an east Indian plant. Use in small quantities as a thickener or stabilizer.

salad dressing simplicity

Chipotle Lime Dressing

INGREDIENTS:

1 package silken-style firm tofu such as Mori-Nu

2 individual chipotle peppers in adobo sauce, (caution - these are hot)

1 fresh lime juice and zest

2 small garlic cloves

1 tsp salt

DIRECTIONS:

Add all ingredients into a food processor or blender. Process until very smooth, scraping down the sides frequently.

["It's never too late to be what you might have been". George Eliot]

Low-Fat Creamy "Caesar" Dressing Dip

INGREDIENTS:

3 cups tofu, silken firm

3/4 cup water

3/4 cup fresh lemon juice

6 Tbsp light soy or chickpea miso

3 Tbsp red wine vinegar

3 Tbsp Dijon mustard

6 cloves garlic, peeled

1 tsp sea salt

1 tsp red pepper

4 dashes pepper hot sauce

DIRECTIONS:

Simply blend all the ingredients in a blender until smooth.

salad dressing simplicity

Simple Dijon Salad Dressing

INGREDIENTS:

1/2 cup red wine vinegar

2 tsp stone ground or Dijon style mustard

1 clove garlic, pressed

1 Tbsp nutritional yeast flakes

1 Tbsp chicken style seasoning

1 Tbsp dried parsley

1 Tbsp dried basil

DIRECTIONS:

Whisk all ingredients together. Use as a dressing for salads and for steamed vegetables.

Ultimate Ranch

INGREDIENTS:

1 cup veganaise

1/2 cup tofutti sour cream

1/3 cup soy milk

2 Tbsp lemon juice

2 Tbsp dill weed

1 Tbsp garlic, fresh minced

1 Tbsp onion powder

1 tsp basil

1 tsp dried bell pepper flakes

DIRECTIONS:

Mix all the ingredients together and refrigerate. Adjusting the thickness is easy just by adjusting the amount of soy milk you use.

soup
simplicity

soup simplicity

There is nothing better than a great bowl of hot soup on a cold winter day, but that's not the only time for soup. We can have soup every day of the year and never have the same soup twice. And it doesn't even need to be hot! There are a lot of cold soups that are struggling their way into the complacent world of hot soup. Cold cherry soup, cold gazpacho soup, and creamy vegetable are just a few. You will even find quite a few soup desserts out there.

By definition soup is a combination of ingredients such as vegetables with a liquid or stock juice. There are a couple main categories of soup that are defined as either clear or thick soups.

Clear soups are generally classified as a bouillon or a consommé. Clear broth soups can get their flavor from a great number of vegetables, herbs, and spices. Even citrus of lemon, lime and orange can give you that secret ingredient that is the wonder of everyone.

Thick soups can be a puree which is thickened with vegetables; a bisque which is made from shellfish, or vegetables thickened with cream; a cream soup which is thickened with béchamel sauces; or a veloute soup which is thickened with eggs, butter and cream. Stews are in a category of their own and are traditionally a much thicker form than a soup.

When it comes to thickening the vegan way there are a couple things you can do. Bean soups can be a watery style bouillon or you can simply mash the beans into a thicker soup.

It is the same concept with pea soup or even potato soup. One thing that you can do to either the bean, potato or pea soup to thicken them, is to add some instant mashed potatoes. And for a creamier version, you can add soy milk.

There is always the cornstarch or arrowroot and water slurry that can thicken most any soup and then we can go with the roux which is a blend of flour and oil formed into a paste. Roux was originally done with just flour and water, but the oil reduces the lumping and has a far less flour taste.

Thickening can also be done with tomato paste, or even ground nuts or flax seeds. Whatever thickening agent you use, you are sure to get a far greater variety of soup textures for your soup experiences.

soup simplicity

Mexican Stew Bread Bowls

INGREDIENTS:

5 medium potatoes, peeled and cubed

3 carrots, chopped

3 stalks celery, chopped

6 cups vegetable broth

1 Tbsp olive oil

1 large onion, diced

4 cloves garlic, minced

1 Tbsp dark chili powder

1 Tbsp cumin

1 1/2 Tbsp seasoned salt

1 (29 ounce) can hominy, drained

1 (28 ounce) can diced tomatoes with green chile peppers

Salt and pepper to taste

DIRECTIONS:

The easiest way to do this recipe is to put everything into a pot, bring to a boil and then low simmer for 1 hour. What I do like to do is sauté the onions in the bottom of the pot with a little bit of olive oil. Wait until they get a brown color and then add all the other ingredients. You can always heat it up a bit more with some red pepper and jalapeno peppers.

For the bread bowls, you will want to cut the tops off the bread and hollow out the bread inside the bottom. Then allow to dry in the open air on the counter overnight. This will keep the bread from being too soggy when adding soup into it.

Curried Tofu Soup

INGREDIENTS:

3 Tbsp vegetable oil

1 Tbsp minced garlic

1/4 cup red curry paste

2 Tbsp dark brown sugar

2 (13.5-ounce) cans light coconut milk

2 1/2 cups vegetable broth

1 lime, juiced

1/4 cup fresh ginger, diced fine

2 Tbsp soy sauce

2 cups carrots, sliced thin

1 1/2 cups green beans, 1 inch cuts

1 (14-ounce) package firm tofu, drained and cut into (1-inch) cubes

3/4 cup fresh cilantro leaves

DIRECTIONS:

Heat oil in a large saucepan over medium-high heat. Add garlic to pan and sauté 30 seconds or until lightly browned. Add curry paste; sauté 1 minute, stirring constantly. Add brown sugar and cook 1 minute. Stir in coconut milk, broth, juice, ginger, and soy sauce. Reduce heat to low; cover and simmer 1 hour. Add carrots, beans, and tofu to pan, and cook for about 10 minutes, just until vegetables are cooked firm. Garnish with cilantro leaves.

soup simplicity

Pumpkin Soup

INGREDIENTS:

1/4 cup water

1 small onion, chopped

4 cups vegetable broth

1 - 16 oz. canned pumpkin

1/2 cup applesauce

2 tsp curry powder

1 tsp pumpkin pie spice

1 tsp fine diced red bell pepper

1 tsp parsley

Several dashes Tabasco pepper sauce

1/2 cup soy or rice milk

DIRECTIONS:

Place the water and onion in a medium saucepan and cook for 5 minutes, until the onions are soft. Add the broth, pumpkin, and applesauce and stir to combine. Add the seasonings and cook over low heat, stirring occasionally, for 10 minutes. Stir in the milk just before serving. Serves about 6

Ten Minute Tuscan White Bean Soup

INGREDIENTS:

2 onions, coarsely chopped

1 Tbsp crushed garlic

Vegetable oil for sauté

1 1/2 cups white beans, pre-soaked

1/2 lb. baby carrots

4 stalks celery, chopped

1 - 8 oz. bag spinach, chopped

2 medium zucchini, chopped

8 oz. fresh mushrooms, chopped

1 quart vegetable broth

5 cups water

2 Tbsp Italian seasoning

Fresh ground pepper to taste

DIRECTIONS:

In a pressure cooker, sauté onions and garlic until soft. Add all other ingredients. Pot will be full, and will all settle down while cooking. Bring to pressure and cook for 5 minutes. Use natural pressure release. Open lid, add pepper – and serve!

soup simplicity

Gingery Split Pea Soup

Chipotle chile provides the essential smokiness while the sliced ginger offers only a background hint of flavor. Cooked to a golden creaminess, the split peas are enhanced with sautéed, almost caramelized, vegetables and finished with a little miso, which contributes its distinctive richness.

INGREDIENTS:

2 cups yellow split peas

2 medium russet potatoes, peeled and diced

2 chipotle chiles, chopped (canned chipotle pepper in adobo sauce)

2 Tbsp fresh ginger, fine chopped

12 cups water

2 tsp sea salt, or to taste

2 medium onions, diced

4 garlic cloves, minced

2 medium carrots, diced

3 celery stalks, diced

2 tsp balsamic vinegar

2 tsp barley

1/2 cup fresh parsley, chopped

DIRECTIONS:

Sauté the onions until brown in color then add garlic and sauté for another minute. Then add all the remaining ingredients except for the parsley and vinegar. Bring to a boil and then simmer for about 1 hour; until peas are completely soft. Mash the peas a little bit to give the soup a little body. Stir in the balsamic vinegar. Taste to adjust salt if necessary. Stir in the chopped parsley and serve hot.

soup simplicity

Butternut Soup

INGREDIENTS:

4 pounds butternut squash, peeled, seeded and chopped

4 large ribs celery, chopped

4 Tbsp olive oil

3 cups thinly sliced leeks, chopped

6 cups vegetable stock

2/3 cup old-fashioned rolled oats

4 tsp Herbs de Provence

1 tsp sea salt

2 Tbsp balsamic vinegar

DIRECTIONS:

In a large soup pot, heat the oil and sauté the leeks for 3 minutes. Add the vegetable stock and bring to a boil. Stir in the squash, celery, oats, Herbs de Provence, and salt and return to a boil. Reduce the heat to medium, cover, and cook at a gentle boil until the squash is very soft, about 15 minutes. Puree the soup with an immersion blender or batch into a food processor and blend until smooth. Stir in enough vinegar to heighten the flavor. Add a bit more salt if needed. Garnish with croutons, and your favorite seeds. You can even drizzle with a little rosemary or basil oil.

African Sweet Potato Soup

INGREDIENTS:

2 Tbsp olive oil

1 large onion, chopped

2 cups cabbage, chopped

3 cloves garlic, minced

18 oz. can sweet potatoes, drained and chopped

14 1/2 oz. can stewed tomato undrained

1 1/2 cups tomato juice

3/4 cup apple juice

2 tsp grated fresh ginger root

1/4 tsp red pepper flakes

2 cups frozen cut green beans

1/3 cup natural peanut butter

DIRECTIONS:

In a large stock pot, heat oil and add the onion, sauté until golden. Mix in the cabbage and garlic and cook until the cabbage is tender-crisp, about 5 minutes. Stir in the remaining ingredients except for the peanut butter, bring to a boil and then low simmer for 30 minutes. Stir in the peanut butter until well-blended and serve. Traditionally, this would be served over rice or mashed potatoes.
Serves 6.

Caribbean Vegetable Stew

INGREDIENTS:

1/4 cup olive oil

1 large onion, chopped

1 red or green bell pepper, chopped

3 cups sweet potatoes, peeled and chopped

1 - 15 ounce can tomato sauce

1 - 15 ounce can diced tomatoes with jalapenos

1 - 20 ounce can pineapple chunks with juice

2 cups green apples unpeeled and chopped

1 - 4 oz. can chopped green chilies

1 cup vegetable broth

1 - 15 ounce can pinto beans, rinsed

1 - 15 ounce can black beans, rinsed

1 - 15 ounce can kidney beans, rinsed

2 Tbsp brown sugar

2 tsp chili powder

1 tsp ground cumin

1 tsp ground oregano

1/2 tsp cinnamon

DIRECTIONS:

Sauté the onion and bell pepper in oil until golden. Add sweet potatoes, tomato sauce, tomatoes, pineapple, apples, chilies and vegetable broth. Bring to a boil, and then low simmer for 45 minutes, stirring occasionally. Add beans and seasonings, mix well and continue to cook over low heat for another 15 minutes, stirring occasionally. Can be served over brown rice or other whole grains. Serves 8-10

crock-pot simplicity

There is nothing better than coming home to an aroma of savory food simmering in the crock-pot. And there is nothing easier than throwing all the ingredients in a crock-pot and flipping a switch.

It's really good to have a notebook in your kitchen to use for crock-potting, this way you can write down what you do every time and continue to make adjustments to flavor, volumes, and temperatures. Make your note changes right after you eat your meal, when it's fresh in your mind, so the next time you make another batch of the same recipe, the notes are already there for you to correct to a consistent perfection.

When it comes to bean crock-potting, fill the crockpot 1/4 to 1/3 full with beans, and then fill the liquids to 1-inch from the top. Beans expand and heat expands so we do want to leave room at the top in order to not be overfilling. Also with beans you may need to add more water later during the cooking process, or try presoaking the beans overnight.

Beans can be served as a soup with the whole beans or you can mash the beans right before serving. This will give you more of a saucy thickness rather than a watery broth. Another way you can do some thickening right before serving is to mix in a little dry mashed potatoes, just a little at a time and continually stirring. When thickening with mash potatoes, keep in mind that it does take a good 2 minutes for the potatoes to come to a full thickness, so don't overdo it. You can also thicken with a cornstarch slurry or roux. One other concept that you will see in a lot of gourmet restaurants is to puree the soups into a smooth texture.

Flavor-wise, let your creativity run wild. Sticking with the savory flavors is good, spicy and salty are generally good for flavor too. I would go on the mild side, and remember that the longer you cook something the saltier it will get. So keep the salt to a bare minimum in the beginning because you can always add a little more later if needed. Citrus can also give you some great flavor and people will be wondering what your secret ingredient is, try throwing in an orange or lime cut in half.

Regardless of how you use your crock-pot, you are guaranteed to have fun, save time and save money too.

Crock-pot Rice Minestrone

INGREDIENTS:

1 medium onion, chopped

2 medium carrots, sliced

2 stalks celery, chopped

1 red bell pepper, diced

1 medium zucchini, scrubbed, sliced into 1/2 inch rounds

2 cloves garlic, minced

2 - 14 1/2 oz. can vegetable broth

1 - 28 oz. can crushed tomatoes

2 - 15 1/2 oz. cans kidney beans, drained

2 tsp dried marjoram

1/4 tsp red pepper

1 1/2 cups cooked rice

DIRECTIONS:

Add all ingredients except rice to crock-pot. Cover and cook on low 8 to 10 hours (high 4 to 5 hours). Add cooked rice and stir to combine. Makes about 8 servings.

crock-pot simplicity

Crock-pot Oil Free Vegan Gumbo

INGREDIENTS:

4 cups vegetable stock

2 cups diced tomatoes

1 cup cooked lima beans

1 1/2 cups sliced okra

1 chopped onion

1 cup corn kernels

1 diced green pepper

1/4 tsp allspice

2 Tbsp minced garlic

2 Tbsp gumbo file

1 tsp salt

DIRECTIONS:

Cover and cook on high for 6 hours (or on low for 8 to 10 hours).

Crock-pot Split Pea

INGREDIENTS:

1 pound dried split peas

1 leek, chopped fine

1 cup celery, chopped fine

1 tsp crushed garlic

7 cups hot water

2 bay leaves

1/4 cup chopped parsley

1 tsp oregano

1 tsp salt to taste

1/2 tsp red pepper to taste

DIRECTIONS:

In a slow cooker, combine all ingredients. Cover and cook on low 7 to 8 hours. Remove bay leaves at end of cooking time. If you like a smoother consistency, puree in a blender or food processor with metal blade. Serve soup in individual bowls. Garnish with chopped parsley.

crock-pot simplicity

Spicy Crock-pot Potato Pea Soup

INGREDIENTS:

2 cups green split peas

8 cups vegetable broth

4 potatoes, chopped

1 cup celery, chopped

2 carrots, sliced

1 onion, diced

2 cloves garlic, minced

1 tsp cumin

1 tsp chili dark powder

1 tsp sage

1 tsp thyme

1 tsp red pepper

Dash pepper sauce

3 bay leaves

3 cups baby red potatoes, diced

1 tsp sea salt and pepper to taste

DIRECTIONS:

Combine all ingredients, except potatoes, in a crock pot. Cover and cook on low for at least 5 hours, or until peas are soft. 1 hour before you are ready to serve, add the diced potatoes. Remove bay leaves and serve.

"If people let government decide what foods they eat and what medicines they take, their bodies will soon be in as sorry a state as *are the souls of those who live* under tyranny."

-Thomas Jefferson

sauce
simplicity

sauce simplicity

Sauce is where you get the flavor for a lot of vegan recipes. I love sauces! It doesn't matter if it's hot or cold, most sauces can be run both ways when it comes to vegan ingredients. There are many names for the sauces, some are called condiments, chutney or salsa, others can be labeled as a gravy, cream or even dressing. It doesn't matter what you call them, they're still part of the sauce family.

> "SAUCES ARE THE *splendor* AND THE *glory* OF FRENCH COOKING"
>
> -Julia Child

Of course Julia Child had a reputation of using a lot of the most unhealthy products on the planet like butter, milk, and cream; but if you're looking for some sauce recipes that are all vegan and taste great, you came to the right book.

TRADITIONALLY, THERE ARE FIVE DIFFERENT TYPES OF SAUCES:

Béchamel: Milk based and thickened with a white roux

Espagnole: Based with a brown stock and thickened with a brown roux

Veloute: A white or clear stock thickened with a blonde roux

Tomate: A tomato based sauce

Hollandaise: An emulsion of eggs, butter, and lemon juice

Today, these sauces can be thickened in many different ways. From these five mother sauces, any secondary sauces can be created and the list is endless as to the thousands of variations imaginable.

And then there is pesto, which was originally referred to the use of a mortar "to grind" with the pestle. It has been called a sauce, when in reality it is a paste; if you were to add it to a veloute or béchamel, then you would have a sauce, but it would still be categorized into the mother sauce and not the pesto.

Sauces are actually a foundation of flavor that you will love to develop into your vegan lifestyle. Sauces don't need to be complicated and many of them are much easier than you think. Some of the greatest sauces are the easiest ones to prepare and when it comes to adding flavor to sandwiches, salads or virtually anything, there is a great easy sauce to compliment it.

sauce simplicity

Here are over 50 of my signature *super fast* favorite sauces:

1000 Island Sauce

Mix:
1 cup veganaise
1 cup ketchup
and 1 cup pickle relish
Thin with pickle juice if desired.

Aioli

Mix:
1/4 cup veganaise
1 tsp fresh lemon juic,
1 tsp fresh cilantro, chopped
1 garlic clove, minced

Simple Tomato Sauce

Sauté 2 cloves diced garlic and one fresh red chile in a splash of olive oil. Add a 1/4 cup of fresh chopped basil and sauté for 1 minute. Add 28 oz. can of chopped tomatoes and simmer for 20 minutes.

Hoisin BBQ Sauce

Cook 3 minced cloves of garlic in olive oil for 1 minute. Stir in: 1/2 cup hoisin sauce
2 tablespoons rice vinegar
2 tablespoons lemon juice
2 tablespoons ketchup
1 tablespoon soy sauce
1 tablespoon sugar
1/3 cup water
Simmer until thickened, cool and then add 1/4 teaspoon sesame oil and 1 chopped scallion.

Cajun BBQ Sauce

Take your favorite BBQ sauce and add 2 tablespoons of cajun seasoning.
Serve cold, or simmer and serve warm.

Root Beer BBQ Sauce

Mix:
1 can of a hearty root beer
1/2 cup ketchup
1/2 cup BBQ sauce
1/4 cup orange juice
2 tablespoons brown sugar
1 tablespoon molasses
1 teaspoon minced ginger
Simmer about 30 minutes until desired thickness, stirring often.

Tangy Steakless Sauce

Take your favorite steak sauce and mix in 2 tablespoons of lemon zest, 1/4 cup molasses, and a 1/4 teaspoon of cayenne pepper.

Red Onion Relish

Cook, until golden:
2 chopped red onions in a skillet with a couple tablespoons of olive oil and and
1/2 teaspoon of salt.
Add 1 clove minced garlic,
1 tablespoon tomato paste,
1/2 cup pitted and chopped kalamata olives, and 1/4 cup orange juice.
Cook until reduced into a relish.

Ginger-Herb Chutney

Pulse puree the following items into a chopped form or blend smooth for a spread:
1/2 cup of each basil, mint, cilantro, and white onion, 1 tablespoon chopped ginger, 1 jalapeno pepper,
1 teaspoon of each, sugar & coriander, and a pinch of salt.
Add a shot of olive oil in the blending as desired.

Fruit Chutney

Mix:
1 cup diced nectarines or peaches, and 1 cup diced papaya.
Add 1/4 red onion, the juice of 1 lime, 1 bunch of chopped cilantro,
1 minced Serrano chile, and a pinch of salt.

sauce simplicity

Green Tomato & Corn Relish

Mix:
2 chopped green green tomatoes
1/2 cup corn
1/2 cup chopped green onions
1/2 cup fine chopped seeded cucumbers
2 tablespoons chopped parsley
2 tablespoons, dijon mustard
and 2 tablespoons cider vinegar

Tofu Relish

Mix:
1 cup fine diced celery
1/2 cup fine diced red onion
1/2 cup firm tofu crumbled
1/4 cup diced fire roasted red pepper
1/4 cup veganaise
1 teaspoon pepper sauce

Walnut Pepper Sauce

Mix:
One cup veganaise
with 1/2 cup extra fine chopped toasted walnuts
1/4 cup diced fire roasted red peppers
1 tablespoon lemon juice
and salt & pepper to taste

The Old Bay Sauce

Mix:
3/4 cup veganaise, zest and juice of 1 lemon
2 teaspoons old bay seasoning
1/4 cup minced green onions and a few drops of pepper sauce.

Peppercorn-Shallot Sauce

Mix:
3/4 cup veganaise, with 1 chopped shallot,
1 tablespoon cracked peppercorns
1 tablespoon fine chopped tarragon, and the juice of 1/2 lemon.
Pinch of salt to taste.

Almond Ancho Sauce

Take 2 dried ancho chilies and soak in 1/2 cup hot water for 30 minutes.
Blend with 3 tablespoons toasted almond slivers, the juice of 1 orange,
1 tablespoon honey, and 4 tablespoons veganaise. Salt optional.

Soy Orange Sauce

Mix well:
1/2 cup orange juice
1 tablespoon natural sugar
2 tablespoons soy sauce
1/4 cup red wine vinegar
dash of sesame oil
sea salt to taste

Balsamic Mustard Sauce

Blend:
1 tablespoon Dijon mustard
1 tablespoon raw Tahini
2 teaspoons balsamic vinegar
1 teaspoon ground flax seed meal

Spiced Peanut Butter Ketchup

Blend:
1 cup ketchup
1/2 cup peanut butter
the juice of 1 lime
1 tablespoon of chili paste
and 1/4 teaspoon of each smoked paprika, allspice, and cayenne

Chinese 5 Spice Ketchup

Mix:
1 cup ketchup with
1 tablespoon Chinese 5 Spice and the juice of one lime.

Curry Ketchup

Brown 1/4 cup fine dices onions in 1 tablespoon olive oil,
add 1 teaspoon curry and one teaspoon paprika and a pinch of cayenne pepper
Toast 1 minute to bring out the flavor then add 1 cup ketchup and 1/2 cup water, and simmer for about 20 minutes until desired thickness.

Cocktail Sauce

Mix:
1 cup ketchup with 1/3 cup horseradish and you're done.
You can bump it up with a shot of lemon juice, Worcestershire, and celery salt. Horseradish has a strong flavor at first, but loses its strength fast when it's not used right away. So start out small and add more as needed.

sauce simplicity

Sun-dried Tomato Ketchup

Puree: 1/2 cup of jarred sun-dried tomatoes with 1 tablespoon cider vinegar, 1 tablespoon brown sugar, and 1/2 cup ketchup.
Blend until desired smoothness.

Roasted Garlic Mustard

Roast 8 cloves of garlic in foil for about 30 minutes at 400 degrees.
Puree garlic with 1/2 cup dijon mustard, 1/4 cup maple syrup, and a pinch of salt and pepper.

Mustard Dill Sauce

Mix:
1/2 cup yellow mustard with 1/4 cup minced onions, 1/8 cup pickle relish, 2 tablespoons fresh chopped dill.

Scallion Ketchup

Mix:
1 cup ketchup with 1/2 cup chopped scallions and 1/4 cup apple juice. Bring to a boil, simmer, and cool.

Jamaican Jerk Ketchup

Mix:
1 cup ketchup with 3 tablespoons of Jamaican jerk seasoning, the juice of 1 lime, and 2 tablespoons of apricot preserves.

Apple Fennel Mustard

Mix:
1/2 cup dijon mustard with 1 apple (peeled and grated),
1 tablespoon apple concentrate, and 1 tablespoon ground fennel.

Peach Time Mustard

Mix:
2 tablespoons of spicy dijon mustard with 1/2 cup peach preserves
1 teaspoon lemon juice
1 teaspoon fresh chopped thyme, and a pinch of salt.

Quick Pico de Gallo

Dice 3 large tomatoes
1 red onion, and 1 jalapeno pepper.
Chop 1 bunch of cilantro
Add a splash of lime juice, and a pinch of salt.

Pineapple Salsa

Mix:
1 cup diced pineapple
1/2 cup diced tomato
1/4 cup diced red onion
1 fine diced jalapeno pepper
1/4 teaspoon allspice, and a pinch of salt.

Roasted Tomato Salsa

Chop 6 plum tomatoes and 1 red onion, spread out on pan and broil for about 7 minutes or until very well browned.
Blend with 1 jared chipotle pepper, 3 tablespoons of fresh cilantro, 1 tablespoon lime, and 2 tablespoons sugar.

Simple Honey Mustard

Mix:
1/2 cup honey with 1/2 cup dijon mustard
To make it creamy, add 1/2 cup veganaise.

Honey Banana Dressing

Blend well 1/2 C water
1 ripe banana
2 tablespoons red wine vinegar
2 tablespoons honey
1 tablespoon dijon grain mustard
1/2 teaspoon cumin
1/4 teaspoon sea salt
pinch red pepper

sauce simplicity

Cucumber Salsa

Mix 1 cup diced seeded cucumber
with 2 diced tomatoes
1/4 cup diced red onion
1 diced jalapeno pepper
1 tablespoon lime juice
2 tablespoons chopped mint
and a pinch of salt

Kraut Sauce

Cook 1/2 cup chopped onion and 1/2 cup rinsed and chopped sauerkraut with 1 tablespoon caraway seeds. Brown with a splash of olive oil. Add 3 tablespoons of veganaise and 3 tablespoons BBQ sauce, and mix.

Miso Ginger Sauce

Mix 4 tablespoons white miso with
3/4 cup veganaise
1 tablespoon fresh grated ginger
and 1 tablespoon honey

Thai Curry Sauce

Mix 1/2 cup veganaise with
1 tablespoon ketchup
2 teaspoons red curry paste
1 tablespoon peanut butter, and
the juice of one lime

Peanut Sauce

Mix 1/3 cup peanut butter, crunchy or smooth
1/2 cup water
2 tablespoons soy sauce
1 tablespoon lime juice
1 clove minced garlic
2 teaspoons grated ginger
1/4 teaspoon red pepper flakes

Avocado-Chile Spread

Puree 1/2 cup vegan sour cream
1 avocado
1/4 cup caned chopped green chiles
1/2 teaspoon crushed garlic, and
the juice of one lime
and a pinch of salt

Chili Sauce

Mix 1/2 cup veganaise with 1/2 cup canned chopped green chilies, 1/2 cup diced green onions, 1/4 cup diced fire roasted red pepper, pinch of salt.

Jalapeno Tartar Sauce

Mix 1 cup veganaise with 1/4 cup chopped pickled jalapenos
1/4 cup chopped green onions
1/4 cup pickle relish
1 tablespoon fresh cut cilantro
1 tablespoon lemon juice

Pickle Sauce

Mix 1 cup veganaise with 1/4 cup chopped dill pickles
1/4 cup pickle relish
1 tablespoon diced fire roasted red bell peppers
1 tablespoon minced red onion
Thin with a few drops of pickle juice.

Wasabi Sauce

Mix 3/4 cup veganaise with 1/2 cup grated cucumber, the juice of 1/2 lemon, 1 tablespoon wasabi paste, and a pinch of salt.

Chipotle Sauce

Puree 2 chipotle peppers with sauce into 1 cup veganaise. Optional add 1/2 cup vegan sour cream or cream cheese for making spreads.

Spicy Duck Sauce

Mix 1/2 cup duck sauce with 3 tablespoons horseradish
2 tablespoons orange marmalade
1 teaspoon rice vinegar
1/2 teaspoon sesame oil
and salt to taste.

sauce simplicity

Quick Cole Slaw Sauce

Mix together:
1 cup veganaise
1/4 cup sugar
1/4 cup vinegar
1 teaspoon black pepper
1 teaspoon celery seed

Basic Vinaigrette

Mix together:
1 cup extra virgin olive oil
1/3 cup good wine vinegar
1 teaspoon sea salt
1/2 teaspoon pepper
Whisk before serving.

Basil Veganaise

Mix:
1 cup veganaise with 1/4 cup basil
1 teaspoon lemon zest and
1 tablespoon lemon juice
Blend in blender till smooth.

Italian Verde Sauce

Mix together:
1/2 cup olive oil
1/3 cup parsley
Zest of 1 lemon
1 tablespoon chopped garlic
1 tablespoon capers
1/2 teaspoon sea salt
pinch of pepper

Blueberry Sauce

Bring to a boil:
3 cups fresh or frozen blueberries
1/3 cup sugar
1/2 cup orange juice
1 tablespoon lemon juice
Thicken with a cornstarch & water slurry.

Zippy Orange Glaze

Mix together:
1 cup orange marmalade
1/4 cup white wine or lemon juice
and add a pinch of cayenne.

Fast Chocolate Sauce

Bring to a boil:
2/3 cup unsweetened cocoa or carob
1 & 1/4 cups water
Allow to cool and add 2 teaspoons of vanilla.

sauce simplicity

Vanilla Sauce

Mix:
1/2 cup sugar with 1 tablespoon cornstarch
Add 1 cup boiling water simmer for 5 minutes until thickened.
Add 2 tablespoons vegan butter, 1 tablespoon vanilla extract and a pinch of salt.

Apple Cider Syrup

Melt 1 tablespoon vegan butter
add 1 cup apple cider
2 cups brown sugar
and 2 cinnamon sticks
Boil to a 50% reduction.
It will thicken as it cools.

Simple Lemon Sauce

Mix:
3/4 cup sugar with 5 teaspoons of cornstarch a pinch of salt and 1 1/2 cups of water, bring to a boil and it will thicken.
Remove from heat and add 1 tablespoon vegan butter, and all the zest and juice from one lemon.

Ultimate Cheese Sauce

INGREDIENTS:

1 cup raw cashews

1 cup pimentos

1/2 cup nutritional yeast flakes

2 Tbsp onion powder

4 Tbsp cornstarch

2 Tbsp lemon juice

1 Tsp salt or to taste

4 cups water, divided

DIRECTIONS:

In a blender, combine all ingredients with only 2 of the cups of water. Blend until mixture is extremely smooth. Transfer mixture to a sauce pan and add the additional 2 cups of water.
Heat on medium until hot and thickened. Adjust water if necessary.

FOR QUESO DIPS:

Take the cheese sauce and add canned diced tomatoes, green chilies, and even salsa.

appetizer
simplicity

As appetizers have become such a huge revenue item for the restaurant industry, it's no wonder that the obesity rates in America have paralleled this trend. For me, many of the appetizers are just the right size for my dinner. Since I have retrained my body to have the biggest meal for breakfast, my dinner is the smallest, and today's appetizers are just about the right size.

So think of appetizers as just another food term for a meal and not to accompany the huge dinner that you shouldn't be having.

Appetizers can be so much fun because we can really go beyond our creative side. It is like the experimental mecca of any culinary passion.

appetizer simplicity

Sweet Potato Fries

INGREDIENTS:

4 large sweet potatoes, cut into wedges or fries

2 Tbsp olive oil

1 tsp cumin

1/4 tsp paprika

1/2 tsp sea salt or to taste

dash red pepper

DIRECTIONS:

Pre-heat the oven to 400 degrees. In a large bowl, toss all ingredients until potatoes are evenly coated with oil and spices. Place potatoes sparingly on a baking sheet and bake for about 30 minutes. I like them to be a light crispy brown, just don't overcook.

I like these fries with BBQ sauce or ketchup, but they are also very popular served with maple syrup.

Ultimate Meatballs

INGREDIENTS:

2 cups oatmeal

2 cups walnuts

2 cups onions, chopped

12 slices whole wheat bread

1 - 16 oz. tofu, firm

1 cup water

1/8 cup soy sauce

2 Tbsp onion powder

2 Tbsp garlic powder

1 Tbsp beefless base

1 tsp basil

1 tsp sage

DIRECTIONS:

Preheat oven to 350 degrees. In a food processor, we are going to blend one ingredient at a time starting with the oatmeal, blend for a couple minutes then add the walnuts and blend for a couple more minutes. Add the bread and blend for another couple minutes, and then add the onions and blend for another couple minutes.

Now you can add all the remaining ingredients and blend well for another few minutes. Using a 1-inch ice-cream scooper, form into balls and place on a sprayed sheet pan. Bake at 350 degrees for about 30 minutes covered and then bake for an additional 10 minutes uncovered to brown the tops a little. Do not overcook, they will dry out fast. These meatballs can now be used for appetizers or for entrees.

dip & salsa
simplicity

In today's world of simplicity it is so easy to produce fabulous dips and salsas for any occasion. The most popular dips are based on three major elements. Texture, flavor, and thickness.

The textures can range from chunky textured salsas to smooth and creamy. Often you may want to incorporate a combination of both.

When it comes to flavor, heat is the trend in many of the recipes of today's style, but you will find that when you tone down the heat, it will bring out the greater flavors of the food. Most of the time the heat actually covers up the flavor of the food and drowns out the great food created. Try more savory flavors, a little salt goes a long way. Citrus lemon, lime and orange will really bring a wow beyond the heat factor.

When it comes to thickness, there are extremes from watery dips to paste style dips. Most dips have a general notion of their thickness so we really try not to go too far out of that complacency. People wouldn't be too happy with a hummus that had the consistency of a syrup dip; regardless of the flavor it presents.

On the other hand when it comes to texture, flavor, and thickness; sometime we can go outside the box to present a really cool variation. It is a simple balance of all three that will bring your dips to the front of the delectable desires of everyone.

I am a true believer in keeping it simple. It's okay to go a little wild on some flavor and you can be a bit more risky when it comes to dips, but do remember that, numbers wise, the farther out you go the more criticism and complaints you will get. Keep your flavors in the zone that everyone will love.

As you search through the sauce simplicity section, you will find a lot of ideas for dips. Here are some more great recipes that can be used as appetizers.

dip & salsa simplicity

Black Bean Salsa

INGREDIENTS:

3 cups chopped tomato (about 2 med.)

1 cup red bell pepper, diced

1 cup green bell pepper, diced

1/2 cup red onion, diced

1/3 cup fresh cilantro, chopped

2 limes, juiced

1/2 tsp salt

1/2 tsp ground cumin

1/2 tsp chili powder

1 jalapeno pepper, finely chopped

1 - 15-ounce can black beans, rinsed and drained

1 - 11-ounce can whole kernel corn, drained

Spicy Orange Cranberry Salsa

INGREDIENTS:

½ cup fresh cranberries

3 navel oranges, zest and chopped

4 Tbsp natural sugar

1 jalapeno, chopped

1 shallot

1 tsp coriander

1/2 tsp cumin

DIRECTIONS:

Place the ingredients in a food processor and pulse until coarsely chopped.

Letting it sit will help the flavors incorporate.

Roasted Corn Guacamole

INGREDIENTS:

1 1/2 cups corn

1/4 cup red onions, diced

3 garlic cloves, minced

2 avocados, halved, pitted, peeled, and cubed

2 tomatoes, chopped

3 Tbsp fresh lime juice

1 tsp chili powder

1/2 tsp chipotle chili powder

3/4 tsp ground cumin

1/2 tsp salt to taste

Preheat the broiler.

DIRECTIONS:

In a bowl, mix together the corn, red onions, and garlic. Spread the vegetable mixture onto a baking pan, and roast in a broiler about 3 inches from the flame for about 8 minutes, stirring often. We want a dark browning and not a burnt product. Remove the pan from the broiler and set aside to cool.

Combine the remaining ingredients in a serving bowl with the corn mixture. Add salt and pepper to taste. Serve immediately or chill and serve later.

Easy Mango Salsa

INGREDIENTS:

2 ripe tomatoes, diced

1 ripe mango, diced

2 Tbsp red onion, chopped

2 Tbsp cilantro, chopped

1 jalapeno chili, seeded & diced

2 Tbsp orange juice

1/2 tsp salt

Toss together and refrigerate up to 6 hours.

Pineapple Salsa

INGREDIENTS:

2 cups pineapple, diced

1 cup Roma tomatoes, chopped

1/2 red onion, diced fine

2 cloves garlic, minced

2 Tbsp jalapeño, diced

2 Tbsp balsamic vinegar

1/4 cup fresh cilantro leaves, chopped

1 tsp extra virgin olive oil

1 lime, juice and zest

1/4 tsp ground cumin

1/4 tsp sea salt

VARIATIONS:

Try combining different tomatoes like sweet grape, yellow, and tomatillos. You can also add a half cup of finely chopped yellow, orange, or green bell peppers, corn, and rinsed black beans.

Tex-Mex Black Bean Dip/Spread

INGREDIENTS:

1 - 15oz. can refried black beans

1/2 cup chopped onion

1/2 cup diced tomato

1/2 cup bottled picante sauce

2 garlic cloves, minced

1/2 tsp chili powder

1/2 tsp ground cumin

1/4 cup fresh cilantro, chopped

1 fresh lime, juiced

Greek Lima Bean Dip

INGREDIENTS:

2 15-ounce cans lima or butter beans drained, but RESERVE LIQUID

2 garlic cloves, minced or pressed

1/4 cup lemon juice

2 Tbsp fresh dill, chopped

1 Tbsp fresh mint, chopped

1/3 cup red onions, chopped

1/4 cup canned diced red pepper

salt and pepper to taste

DIRECTIONS:

In a food processor, puree the limas, garlic, lemon juice, dill and mint. If needed, add about 1/4 cup or more of the reserved bean liquid to aid in pureeing and process until smooth and creamy. Fold in the red onions and red pepper by hand and add salt and pepper to taste. Serve at room temperature, or chill and serve cold.

hummus
simplicity

hummus simplicity

Hummus has certainly gained popularity over the past few years and it is no coincidence that it is extremely healthy and easy to prepare. The variety of hummus creations are endless.

Traditionally, hummus has been around since the 13th century when it was a cold puree of chickpeas with vinegar, pickled lemons, herbs, spices, and oil. There was no tahini in the recipes of yesterday until the 19th century. The main history of the word is Arabic and derived from the word "chickpeas"

Nutritionally hummus is full of iron, vitamin C, and vitamin B6. It also is high in protein at eight grams per 3.5 oz. serving.

Today's hummus recipes generally consist of the chickpeas blended with tahini, which is a ground sesame paste, olive oil, lemon juice, garlic, and salt. The olive oil has only recently been introduced to hummus recipes, originally it was just pureed with lemon juice and water. Blending without the oil is actually recommended, especially for those reducing their oil content. Adding oil to your hummus literally adds huge additions of calories to your recipes. The whole concept is to blend the chickpeas into a smoothness and oil certainly does help, but you can achieve the same effect with water or different juices.

Regardless of how you make your hummus, you're sure to become a pro at creating these simple solutions to healthy eating. Here are some great starter recipes to guide you in your hummus development.

Spicy Red Pepper Hummus

INGREDIENTS:

2 cloves garlic, peeled

2 - 16-ounce cans cooked chickpeas

Cooking liquid from the beans (or water)

1 lemon, juice and zest

2 Tbsp tahini

1/2 tsp cumin

1 tsp red pepper

1/4 tsp chipotle chili powder

salt (to taste)

10 ounce jar of diced roasted red peppers for sprinkling on top

Black Bean Hummus

INGREDIENTS:

3 cups cooked black beans

4 Tbsp cooking liquid from beans or more

4 Tbsp lemon juice or more if needed

2 clove garlic, peeled

2 Tbsp tahini

1 tsp ground cumin

1/2 tsp salt

1/4 tsp cayenne pepper

hummus simplicity

Spinach Hummus

INGREDIENTS:

1 - 16 oz. can chickpeas with juice

3 cloves garlic

2 Tbsp tahini

1/4 cup lemon juice

1/4 tsp cayenne

6 oz. fresh spinach

pinch of salt

Black Olive Hummus

INGREDIENTS:

2 16 oz. can cooked chickpeas, drained

4 Tbsp water

2/3 cup fresh lemon juice

2 tsp salt

1/2 cup black olives, diced

Simple Hummus

INGREDIENTS:

2 cloves garlic

1 - 16oz. can chickpeas, not drained

1/8 cup lemon juice

1 Tbsp tahini

salt to taste

pinch cayenne

a few sprigs fresh parsley

Low Fat Red Pepper Hummus

INGREDIENTS:

1 - 16oz. can chickpeas with juice

2 Tbsp tahini

1 Tbsp lemon juice

3 cloves garlic chopped

1/2 cup roasted red peppers

1 1/2 tsp cumin

1 tsp coriander

1/2 tsp cayenne

1/2 tsp salt

Walnut-Flaxseed Hummus

INGREDIENTS:

1 - 16-ounce can cooked chickpeas, drained

2 cloves garlic, peeled

1/4 cup walnuts

1 Tbsp ground flaxseeds

1/4 cup water

1/8 cup lemon juice

1/4 tsp ground cumin

1/4 tsp paprika

Dash red pepper

bruschetta
simplicity

bruschetta simplicity

Bruschetta is an all-time favorite that can be served as an appetizer, a side, or even as a meal. It can be served hot or cold. Traditionally, it was a butter toasted bread with a topping of tomatoes, garlic and spice.

One of the most practical ways to make bruschetta is to broil the bread with a light coat of olive oil and no toppings whatsoever, we will top it later. Any bread will work, but is most often done with a french baguette. You can also grill the bread in a pan if you like. The reason you want to do a grilling with oil and no toppings whatsoever is that water and oil don't mix. When you do a quick searing of the oil on the bread, it will resist the moisture in the toppings from being able to penetrate into the bread. The last thing you want is a soggy bread that is falling apart. I would recommend also keeping the topping well drained, we don't want to squeeze every flavor out of the tomatoes and toppings, but we do want to keep it on the drier side.

Topping can consist of virtually anything, don't let your mind be limited to the traditions of man and tomatoes. Try vegetables of every kind, just make sure that they are a softened vegetable and not too crunchy. You can also do a great number of fruits, but make sure not to over cook them into a watery state that will make the bread soggy.

Toasting the bread with the toppings on top is a great way to warm up the toppings and give it a nice finish. The hotter the oven, the more browning you will be doing. Adding some vegan cheese to the top and browning is a nice compliment to many bruschetta.

Flavors can run in many directions, salty, and savory are great, but try some tart or sweet, even an element of bitter can really round out an amazing flavor.

bruschetta simplicity

Avocado Mango Bruschetta

INGREDIENTS:

2 Tbsp olive oil

1 avocado, ripe but firm (peeled pitted, and diced)

1 cup fresh mango, diced

1/4 cup red bell pepper, diced

2 Tbsp fresh basil, chopped

1 Tbsp lime juice

Salt & pepper to taste

bruschetta simplicity

Mushroom Bruschetta

INGREDIENTS:

3 Tbsp olive oil

3 cloves garlic

1 lb. mixed mushrooms, chopped & sauteed

1/4 cup fresh parsley, chopped

1 Tbsp thyme

Salt & pepper.

Simple Bruschetta Topping

INGREDIENTS:

4 Roma tomatoes, chopped

1/4 red onion, thinly diced

1 clove garlic, finely minced

Splash olive oil

Pinch Salt

Pinch Red Pepper,

Pinch Basil

Pinch Oregano

Balsamic & Sun-dried Bruschetta

INGREDIENTS:

6 Roma tomatoes, chopped

1/2 cup sun-dried tomatoes, packed in oil

3 cloves minced garlic

1/4 cup olive oil

3 Tbsp balsamic vinegar

1/4 cup fresh basil, stems removed

1/4 tsp salt

Pinch ground red pepper

grilling
simplicity

grilling simplicity

One of my favorite passions is to do some outdoor grilling. Far too often we see the vegan mentality drawing away from the char-broiler. Well if there is no steak or chicken, what's the point? Well the point is flavor, and the flavor that we get from the grilling is the most popular flavor in the history of the world. In fact putting food over an open flame was the first form of cooking thousands of years ago, and we have been doing it ever since. It makes for great entrees and appetizers alike.

So the big question is what to grill? And the big answer is anything! You can even grill applesauce, yeah applesauce!! It's really great to core up some apples and place them in a pan, with a little water bath, atop a mesquite chip smoking BBQ. You can actually make the best flavored stuffed apples with raisins and caramel. And even later, puree them into the greatest applesauce. I always like to have some type of pan on the cool zone that is absorbing the flavors.

Dive into the many flavors that go so well with the grilling normality like BBQ sauces, teriyaki sauces, or marinades. Do be careful with the sugar based sauces for they have a greater burning risk. I also recommend the dustings with steak or chicken seasonings and mesquite or hickory flavored dustings. These products intended for meat are actually great flavor additions for vegetable grilling.

Most of the grilling you will enjoy, is the grilled vegetables and tofu. Whether you do k-bobs or right on the grill, it's a sure hit. You don't even have to add one single spice and people will love them. If you do the plain grilling, I do recommend having a clean grill, and spray the grill and/or food with a little oil spray. This will help prevent any sticking.

Another secret to great grilling is to not start grilling too soon. Let the grill get heated up first. If it gets too hot and you're already cooking, don't panic. You can always get your markings and flavor from the char-broiler and then shift the food to a cool zone to finish it off, or finish the cooking in the oven.

Always keep a supply of mesquite, hickory and apple chips on hand. If you are doing a fast grilling time, you can put these chips on the charcoal dry, and for longer cooking times just soak in hot water for a few minutes before use. For gas grills, there is usually an area to place the flavor chip. I put the chips in a drip pan right on a direct flame. It really works great if you can drill a bunch of holes in the pan.

I also like to grill a lot of vegetables for the next few days. It is great to grill sliced zucchini, eggplant, onions and peppers, for later use. They make great wraps hot or cold, add them to salads, or layer them atop a casserole for that finishing wow factor.

Another great thing to do since you have the char-broiler on, is to do some whole fire roasted red bell peppers. Just place the red peppers on the grill and turn a few times until the entire pepper is grilled to a medium dark brown. Then the easiest thing to do is place them into a zip-lock baggie until they cool. This will make them sweat and enable you to skin them with an extreme ease. These peppers can be chilled for a good week, and for a longer shelf life, salt and oil, or vinegar can be used.

Once you start grilling this way, you will be wondering why you never did this before.

Don't forget that grilling sandwiches with a little vegan cheese and veggies, you can turn a simple sandwich into a masterpiece. The panini machines are nice, but if you don't have one, don't worry; you can do the same thing on the grill, just remember to keep it on the cooler side of the grill and not in the hot zone.

Wraps are great on the grill too. It will not only give it the visual appeal, it adds to the flavor and can take a cold wrap to a whole new dimension.

grilling simplicity

Simple Vegetable Grilling

VEGETABLES:

1 large red onion, large dice

1 large yellow squash, 3/4 inch slices

1 large green zucchini, 3/4 inch slices

1 eggplant, 1 inch slices

1 red bell pepper, wedges

1 lb. large mushrooms, quartered

MIX:

1/4 cup olive oil

1 Tbsp garlic, minced

1/2 tsp fresh rosemary, chopped

1/4 tsp red pepper

1/2 tsp salt, or to taste

DIRECTIONS:

Mix all the vegetables with the spices and oil together well, then grill to perfection. These can also be done in the oven on a broil setting.

NOTE:
From this simplicity, you can change, add and modify all of your vegetables, spices, oils, and flavors.

Grilled Spinach & Sun-dried Tomato Pizza

That's right, grilled pizza! This is a great recipe for a char-broiler that is primed with mesquite chips. The smoke flavor will impress even the biggest critics.

INGREDIENTS:

- 1 pizza dough pre-made or fresh made
- 4 Tbsp olive oil
- 1 tsp garlic, minced
- 1/4 tsp oregano
- 1/4 tsp thyme
- 1/4 tsp rosemary
- 1 cup vegan cheese
- 1 cup fresh spinach leaves
- 1 cup sun-dried tomatoes, whole or sliced
- 1/2 cup tofu
- 4 Tbsp vegetable broth
- 1/4 tsp liquid smoke

DIRECTIONS:

Prepare pizza dough as desired, I prefer to make it fresh but the pre-made will do, it will just have a quicker cooking time. Coat pizza with the olive oil, garlic and spices, then top with the vegan cheese, spinach and sun-dried tomatoes.

For the tofu crumble topping, press a slice of whole tofu with a plate for a little time to remove the water content then crumble the tofu and soak with a blend of vegetable broth liquid smoke. Add to the topping.

For the grilled pizza, I add some mesquite chips to the fire. Placing the pizza on 2 stacked pizza pans will prevent the bottom from getting too done. Close the cover and cook the pizza for about 15 minutes or until crisp and browned. I like to have a cooking temperature of 400 to 450 degrees. As grilling temperatures vary so does the cooking time.

Simple Dough Recipe

INGREDIENTS:

- 1 - 25 oz. package dry active yeast
- 1 cup warm water
- 2 cups high gluten flour
- 2 Tbsp olive oil
- 1 tsp salt
- 2 tsp natural sugar

DIRECTIONS:

In a small bowl, dissolve yeast in warm water. Let rest until creamy, about 10 minutes. In a large bowl, combine 2 cups bread flour, olive oil, salt, white sugar and the yeast mixture; stir well to combine. Knead well until a dough has formed. Cover and allow to rise until doubled in volume, about 30 minutes.

Place dough out onto a well floured area and form into a pizza crust shape. Now it's ready to cover with any toppings.

Grilled Chili-Lime Sweet Potatoes

INGREDIENTS:

4 large sweet potatoes

2 limes, juice and zest

3 Tbsp of sesame oil

1 tsp of chili pepper

2 cloves of garlic, minced

1/2 tsp sea salt

DIRECTIONS:

Light the grill. Bring a 6-quart container 1/2 full of water to a boil. Cut sweet potatoes into wedges and boil for about 5 minutes, until tender but still firm. Remove from heat, drain and put into the freezer for about 5 minutes.

Combine the remaining ingredients in a large bowl and pour over potatoes like a marinade. Let rest for 15 minutes lightly tossing on occasion.

Grill the potatoes on medium to high heat. Flip and rotate until the potatoes start to crisp and the glaze is blackened a bit. Remove from heat. Sprinkle with salt if desired and serve hot; plain or with sauce, they're great.

Spice Grilled Tofu

INGREDIENTS:

1 lb. extra firm tofu, drained and cut lengthwise into 6 slices

1/2 cup fresh lime juice

1/2 cup maple syrup

1/4 cup soy sauce

2 tsp chili paste

1 Tbsp garlic, minced

1/4 tsp red pepper

DIRECTIONS:

Drain and press down the tofu with a plate to squeeze out the water. Place the tofu flat in the bottom of a baking dish.

In a small bowl, whisk together the lime juice, maple syrup, soy sauce, chili paste, garlic, and pepper. Pour mixture over and under the tofu, to coat all the slices. Cover the baking dish with plastic wrap and place in the refrigerator for at least 4 hours or overnight.

For cooking, heat char-broiler or grill pan to medium heat. Spray grill with nonstick cooking spray. Place tofu slices on the grill, saving the marinade. Grill tofu 3 or 4 minutes on each side, or until the outside is browned and crisp. Return tofu to the baking dish and toss the slices with the reserved marinade. Serve immediately.

Cajun Grilled Tofu

This cajun recipe kicks tofu up a couple of notches for sure! It couldn't be quicker or easier to make, and the results work beautifully as a low-fat, low-carb, high-protein, abundantly flavorful main dish—or as a zesty topping for salad.

All it takes is some tofu and a fabulous Creole Seasoning Rub, recipe included. And if you don't feel like firing up the grill, we've included the just-as-easy skillet directions.

INGREDIENTS:

1 pound extra-firm tofu, drained

1/2 cup vegetable oil

2 Tbsp Cajun Seasoning Rub (recipe below)

DIRECTIONS:

Press the excess water out of the tofu. Cut into 3/4 inch thick slices and place in a baking dish. In a mixing bowl, stir together the vegetable oil and the seasoning. Brush mixture over both sides of the tofu, cover with plastic wrap, and refrigerate for 4 hours or overnight. Lightly coat grill with oil and grill tofu over medium-high heat, turning once, until golden brown on both sides. Reserved marinade can be drizzled over tofu before serving.

Cajun Seasoning Rub

INGREDIENTS:

3 Tbsp sea salt

1 1/2 tsp sweet paprika

1 Tbsp onion powder

1 Tbsp cayenne pepper

1/2 tsp white pepper

2 tsp dried thyme

1 tsp dried oregano

grilling simplicity

Lemon Achiote Grilled Tofu Recipe

INGREDIENTS:

1 package of extra firm tofu

1/3 cup fresh squeezed lemon juice

2 Tbsp achiote powder (available in Mexican markets)

3 cloves garlic, minced

1 Tbsp brown sugar

1 Tbsp cilantro, minced

1/4 tsp cayenne pepper

1/4 tsp sea salt

DIRECTIONS:

Press the excess water out of the tofu. Cut into 3/4 inch thick slices and place in a baking dish. In a mixing bowl, stir together the remaining ingredients for a marinade. Brush mixture over both sides of the tofu, cover with plastic wrap, and refrigerate for 4 hours or overnight. Lightly coat grill with oil and grill tofu over medium-high heat, turning once, until golden brown on both sides. Reserved marinade can be drizzled over tofu before serving.

Grilled Peach Cobbler

Even though this is a dessert, its flavor is really enhanced because of the char-broiler smoking. I really love to make sure the apple or hickory chips are smoking well.

INGREDIENTS:

- 6 to 8 ripe peaches
- 1/4 cup vegan margarine, melted & divided
- 1/4 cup brown sugar, divided
- 2 tsp ground cinnamon, divided
- 1 cup granola

DIRECTIONS:

Heat the grill to medium high. Take the peaches, cut in half removing the pit, then slice them large enough not to fall through the grill. Place the peaches on the grill until browned and flip. Remove from the grill and cool.

In one mixing bowl, mix peaches with 1/2 of the cinnamon, brown sugar and vegan margarine. Then place into a baking dish. In another bowl, mix the granola with the remaining butter, sugar and cinnamon and sprinkle on top of the peaches. Place the dish onto the grill, close the cover, and bake until the granola is golden brown, 15 to 20 minutes. Serve with vegan ice cream or peach sorbet.

sandwich simplicity

sandwich simplicity

You can make thousands of sandwiches from the veggies we have available to us every day. I often go to Subway when I am on the road and get a veggie sub on 9-grain honey oat bread, no cheese, no meat, just loaded with all the great veggies and then I bump it up a little bit with the sweet onion sauce. At home, the veggie combinations are endless, especially when you carry a variety of breads, wrap tortillas, and pitas. Some people will even go gluten free and actually make a wrap with green leaf lettuce.

As you can see once again, going vegan is so much easier than any other type of cooking. Here are some great suggestions that need no recipe to produce. I do also recommend having fun with the sauces and spreads because that will be the defining flavor to compliment any veggie sandwich.

BBQ Jack Fruit Sandwiches

This is the vegan of all vegan recipes! If you are looking for a simple recipe to really blow away any meat lover, then make these mock pork sandwiches.

INGREDIENTS:

2 cans green jack fruit

1 jar favorite BBQ sauce

DIRECTIONS:

Take the jack fruit and hand pull apart into strands. This will simulate a pulled pork look. Boil the fruit in enough water to be covered, for about 25 minutes. Drain and add your favorite BBQ sauce, bring to a boil and it's done. Serve atop buns, make into wraps, stuff baked potatoes; the list is long as to the creativity this product will bring.

NOTE: You can find green jack fruit in any Asian food store.

["Whether *you think you can* or think you can't, you are right".

-Henry Ford]

sandwich simplicity

Mock Egg Salad Sandwiches

INGREDIENTS:

1 block firm tofu, drained

1/3 cup veganaise

1/3 cup sweet relish

1/2 tsp lemon juice

1/2 stalk celery, diced

1 Tbsp prepared mustard

1/2 tsp garlic powder

1/2 tsp onion powder

1/4 tsp salt to taste

DIRECTIONS:

In a medium-sized bowl, mash the tofu with a fork. Add remaining ingredients and stir together until well combined. Sprinkle with paprika for garnish, if desired.

Eggless Egg and Garden Veggie Salad

INGREDIENTS:

1 block firm tofu, pressed and crumbled

1/2 cup veganaise

1/2 cup carrots, shredded

1/2 cup red bell pepper, diced fine

1/2 cup celery, diced fine

1/4 cup green onions, sliced fine

1/4 cup freshly chopped parsley

1 1/2 tsp lemon juice

1 tsp onion powder

3/4 tsp garlic powder

1/2 tsp salt

1/4 tsp turmeric

1/8 tsp red pepper

DIRECTIONS:

Combine all ingredients and let rest for a couple minutes, then mix again. This will help the flavors and turmeric color incorporate through the salad.

sandwich simplicity

Easy Black Bean Sloppy Joe

INGREDIENTS:

1 onion, chopped

1 red pepper, diced

1/3 cup water

1 15-ounce can black beans, rinsed

1 8-ounce can tomato sauce

1/4 cup quick oatmeal

1/3 cup BBQ sauce

2 Tbsp soy sauce

1 Tbsp yellow mustard

1 tsp natural sugar

1 tsp chili powder

DIRECTIONS:

Place onion & pepper in saucepan with water and soy sauce. Cook until the vegetables soften, about 5 minutes.

Mash beans for a couple minutes, leaving a chunky mashed look. Add the beans and remaining ingredients into the saucepan and cook over low heat until heated, about 5 minutes. Serve on buns.

Chicken-less Chicken Salad

INGREDIENTS:

1 brick tofu, extra firm

Soy sauce for marinating

3 ribs celery, diced

1 small red onion, diced

1 red pepper, diced

1/2 tsp each basil, sage, rosemary, oregano (or to taste)

2 tsp paprika

1-1 1/2 cup Tofu Spread (see below)

DIRECTIONS:

Preheat oven to 400 degrees. Slice tofu 1/4 inch thick and brush both sides with soy sauce and place flat on a lightly oiled baking sheet. Let marinate for 10 minutes and brush again. Bake for 30-35 minutes, turning once halfway through, until golden brown and crispy on the outside and still tender on the inside. Allow to cool, then shred the tofu slices with a knife, creating irregular pieces appearing to be shredded chicken. Mix with vegetables, spices and tofu spread until ingredients are well-incorporated. Chill thoroughly before serving.

This is a great item for salads as well as sandwiches, or even served with crackers as an appetizer.

Simple Tofu Spread

INGREDIENTS:

1 - 12 oz. brick silken tofu

3 Tbsp stone ground mustard

3 Tbsp brown rice syrup

2 Tbsp cider vinegar

1/4 tsp sea salt to taste

1 lemon, juiced

DIRECTIONS:

Puree all ingredients in a food processor until smooth and creamy. You will love this tofu spread for a lot of different applications.

burger
simplicity

Black Bean Thai Burger

INGREDIENTS:

1 - 16 oz. can refried black beans

1/2 green bell pepper, chopped

1/2 onion, chopped

1/2 cup bread crumbs

3 cloves garlic, chopped

3 egg replacer of ground flax seed and water

3 Tbsp Thai chili sauce

1/2 Tbsp chili powder

1/2 Tbsp cumin

DIRECTIONS:

In a food processor, finely chop bell pepper, onion, and garlic. In a small bowl, stir in chili powder, cumin, and chili sauce. Mix all together with breadcrumbs until the mixture is sticky and holds together. Divide mixture into four patties.

NOTE: If grilling, preheat an outdoor grill for high heat, place patties on lightly oiled foil, and grill about 8 minutes on each side.

If baking, preheat oven to 375 degrees, place patties on lightly oiled baking sheet, and bake about 10 minutes on each side.

burger simplicity

Portobello Burgers

INGREDIENTS:

4 large portobello mushroom caps

MARINADE:

1/4 cup low-sodium soy sauce

1/4 cup balsamic vinegar

2 Tbsp olive oil

3 garlic cloves, minced

RED BELL VEGANAISE SAUCE:

1/2 red bell pepper fire, fire roasted then minced

1/4 cup veganaise

1/2 tsp olive oil

1/8 tsp ground red pepper

Pinch sea salt to taste

DIRECTIONS:

Marinade mushrooms for at least 2 hours and they are ready to grill. I often do the marinating in a plastic bag and then just shake around a couple times.

Preheat grill to medium heat. Place mushrooms, gill sides down, on grill rack coated with cooking spray; grill about 5 minutes on each side. Serve with toasted bun and your favorite condiments.

Lentil-Barley Burgers with Fiery Fruit Salsa

INGREDIENTS:

Salsa:

1/4 cup finely chopped pineapple

1/4 cup finely chopped mango

1/4 cup finely chopped tomatillo

1/4 cup halved grape tomatoes

1 Tbsp fresh lime juice

1 Serrano chili, minced

DIRECTIONS:

For the salsa:
Combine ingredients, cover and refrigerate.

BURGER INGREDIENTS:

- 1 1/2 cups water
- 1/2 cup dried lentils
- 1 cup onion, minced
- 1/4 cup grated carrot
- 1 Tbsp garlic, minced
- 3 Tbsp tomato paste
- 1 1/2 tsp ground cumin
- 3/4 tsp dried oregano
- 1/2 tsp chili powder
- 3/4 tsp sea salt
- 3/4 cup cooked pearl barley
- 1/2 ++ cup panko Japanese breadcrumbs
- 1/4 cup finely chopped fresh parsley
- 1/2 tsp red pepper
- 2 egg replacer of ground flax seed and water

DIRECTIONS:

For the burgers: If barley needs to be cooked, cook and chill. Cook lentils with 1 1/2 cups water, and bring to a boil. Cover, reduce heat, and simmer about 25 minutes or until lentils are tender. Drain and place half of lentils in a large bowl. Place other half in a food processor and process until smooth. Add processed lentils to whole lentils in the bowl.

In a large nonstick skillet over medium-high heat, sauté carrots and onions for about 6 minutes, until tender. Add garlic and cook additional 2 minutes, stirring constantly. Add tomato paste, cumin, oregano, chili powder, and sea salt; cook another 2 minutes, stirring constantly. Add onion mixture to lentils, along with the remaining ingredients, stir well. Add more panko if needed to bind together. Cover and refrigerate 1 hour or until firm.

Divide mixture into 8 portions, shaping each into 1/2-inch thick patties. Sauté with a little vegetable oil on medium-high heat. Cook for about 4 minutes on each side or until browned. Serve with salsa topping.

Grilled Lemon-Basil Tofu Burgers

INGREDIENTS:

1 pound firm or extra firm tofu, pressed & sliced into 4 slices

LEMON MARINADE:

1/3 cup finely chopped fresh basil

1/4 cup fresh lemon juice

2 cloves garlic, minced

2 Tbsp Dijon mustard

2 Tbsp honey

1 Tbsp olive oil

2 tsp lemon rind

1/2 tsp salt

1/4 tsp red pepper

PREPARATION:

In a small bowl, combine lemon marinade ingredients. Cut tofu crosswise into 4 or 5 slices. Place tofu slices on a sheet pan and brush both sides of tofu slices with lemon juice mixture; reserve remaining juice mixture. Let tofu rest 1 hour or more.

Preheat grill to a medium high heat. Place tofu slices on grill rack coated with cooking spray. Grill for about 4 minutes on each side. Brush tofu with the reserved juice mixture.

Olive relish is a great compliment to these tofu burgers. I also enjoy lettuce, tomato, and red onion slices.

OLIVE RELISH:

1/3 cup finely chopped pitted kalamata olives

2 cloves garlic, minced

3 Tbsp vegan sour cream

3 Tbsp veganaise

burger simplicity

Vegetable Burgers

INGREDIENTS:

1 cup garbanzo beans, rinsed

1 cup fresh cilantro, chopped

1/2 cup carrot, chopped

1 Tbsp jerk rub

1 tsp sea salt

1/2 tsp red pepper

1 jalapeno, chopped

2 pounds peeled red potatoes, cut into 2-inch pieces

1/4 cup red onion

1 cup dry bread crumbs

PREPARATION:

Combine first 7 ingredients in the bowl of a food processor; process until finely chopped.

Boil potatoes and onion until tender, drain and cool. Place potato mixture in a bowl and mash. Stir in chickpea mixture and bread crumbs, then cover and chill 8 hours or overnight.

Divide potato mixture into 8 equal portions, shaping each portion into a 1/2-inch-thick patty. Pan fry on medium-high with a little vegetable oil for about 5 minutes on each side and they are ready to serve with all your burger condiments.

247

Black Bean and Lentil Burgers with Pickled Carrots and Radishes

INGREDIENTS:

For the Burgers:

1 cup cooked lentils

1/2 red onion, quartered

3 garlic cloves, chopped

1/4 cup cornmeal

1/2 cup wheat bran or wheat germ

2 tsp ground cumin

1 tsp chile powder

1 tsp sea salt

1/2 cup packed cilantro

1 carrot, shredded

2 cups cooked black beans

DIRECTIONS FOR THE BURGERS:

In a food processor, pulse the onion and garlic until minced. Add in the cornmeal, wheat bran, cumin, chili powder, sea salt, and cilantro. Pulse a few more times until everything is well combined. Place this mixture into a large bowl and stir in the shredded carrot.

Place the black beans and cooked lentils in the processor bowl. Blend until the beans and lentils are smooth. Place into the same bowl as the onion mixture and mix well.

Divided the mixture into 8 equal portions and shape into patties. Make them thick enough so they don't fall apart easily, no less than 1/2-inch thick.

Grill the burgers for about 6 to 7 minutes on each side or until browned and grill marks start to show. You can also cook them in a skillet. Serve with the pickled carrots and radishes and all your other favorite fixings.

The burgers can be made a day ahead and stored covered in the fridge before cooking and serving. You can also freeze the patties, tightly wrapped and sealed, for up to a month. Makes 6 to 8 patties, depending on size.

burger simplicity

INGREDIENTS FOR THE PICKLED CARROTS AND RADISHES:

1 large carrot, extra fine sliced no thicker than 1/8-inch

1/2 bunch radishes, extra fine sliced no thicker than 1/8-inch

1 Tbsp salt

1 Tbsp natural sugar

1/2 tsp red pepper flakes

1/4 cup rice vinegar

DIRECTIONS FOR THE PICKLED VEGGIES:

Place the carrots and radishes in a small bowl and toss with the salt. Let sit for 10 minutes. You should see some liquid in the bottom of the bowl and the veggies will be slightly softer. Rinse off the veggies and allow to drain.

Place back in the bowl, add the sugar, chili peppers, and the vinegar. Allow to sit for at least 2 hours for maximum flavor. You can make this ahead of time and keep covered in the fridge.

Corn & Bean Burgers with Chipotle Ketchup

BURGER INGREDIENTS:

2 Tbsp olive oil

1 - 15 oz. can kidney beans, rinsed

1 - 15 oz. can black beans, rinsed

1/3 cup dry bread crumbs

1/4 cup canned whole-kernel yellow corn, drained

1/4 cup onion, diced

2 egg replacer of ground flax seed and water

CHIPOTLE KETCHUP:

1/3 cup ketchup

1 tsp honey

1 tsp lime juice

1 Tbsp juice from canned chipotle chilies

1/2 tsp ground cumin

BURGER DIRECTIONS:

In a large bowl, combine kidney beans and black beans and partially mash with a fork. Add the bread crumbs, corn, onion, and egg replacer. Mix until well blended and holding together. Form bean mixture into 1/2 inch thick patties. Cook on medium-high heat for about 5 minutes on each side or until crisp and beginning to brown.

CHIPOTLE KETCHUP:

Mix all ingredients well and it's ready.

burger simplicity

Hominy-Pinto Burgers with Roasted Poblano Chilies

INGREDIENTS:

2 poblano chilies

BURGER INGREDIENTS

1 cup chopped onion

2 garlic cloves, minced

1/4 tsp salt

1 - 15 oz. can pinto beans, rinsed

1 - 15 oz. can hominy, rinsed

1/2 cup masa

SALSA CREAM

2 Tbsp vegan sour cream

2 Tbsp salsa

Mix well.

DIRECTIONS:

For the Chilies: Preheat broiler. Place chilies on a foil-lined baking sheet; broil 3 inches from top of broiler until blackened and charred. Flip and repeat. Place in a plastic bag and let sweat for 10 minutes. Peel and discard skins. Cut each chili lengthwise into 4 strips; discard seeds.

For the Burgers: Sauté onion and garlic for 5 minutes until dark golden. Place onion mixture, salt, beans, and hominy in a food processor; pulse until choppy to fine ground. Combine bean mixture and 1/2 cup masa. Divide mixture into 4 equal portions, shaping each into 1/2 inch patties. With 1/4 cup masa in a shallow dish we are going to dredge the patties until well dusted.

Cook patties for about 5 minutes on each side. Top patties with a slice of roasted chili and salsa cream.
These are great burgers for ciabatta bread. Serve with choice of condiments.

Quick & Simple Black Bean Burger

INGREDIENTS:

1 cup bread crumbs (fresh, not dried)

3 Tbsp olive oil, divided

2 tsp chopped garlic

1 - 15 oz. can black beans, rinsed

1 tsp grated lime zest

3/4 tsp chili powder

1/2 tsp chopped fresh oregano

1/4 tsp salt

2 egg replacer ground flax seed & water

DIRECTIONS:

Fresh bread crumbs can be made by placing some slices of bread in a processor and pulsing for a moment. Remove bread crumbs and place into bowl.

Combine 1 tablespoon olive oil, garlic, and beans in processor; pulsing until it makes a thick paste. Scrape bean mixture into bowl and add bread crumbs. Stir in lime zest and remaining ingredients. With moistened hands, divide bean mixture into 4 equal portions. Make patties about 3/4 inch thick.

Oil burgers lightly and pan fry or BBQ over medium to medium-high heat. Cook for 4 to 5 minutes or until bottom edges are browned. Carefully turn patties over and cook another 4 minutes.

Open-Faced Falafel Burgers

BURGER INGREDIENTS:

1 cup chopped red onion

1/2 cup fresh cilantro, chopped

2 Tbsp lemon juice

1 tsp cumin

1 tsp ground coriander

1/2 tsp sea salt

2 - 15 oz. cans garbanzo beans, drained

4 garlic cloves, minced

1/2 ++ cup dry bread crumbs, divided

SAUCE INGREDIENTS:

1/2 cup water

1/2 cup vegan sour cream

1/4 cup tahini

3 Tbsp fresh lemon juice

1/8 teaspoon salt

2 garlic cloves, minced

BURGER PREPARATION:

Combine all the burger ingredients except the bread crumbs. Process until smooth. Place bean mixture in a large bowl and stir in 1/4 cup bread crumbs. Mix and add more bread crumbs if needed to achieve desired binding. Divide bean mixture into 6 equal portions, shaping each into a 1/2-inch patty. Place remaining 1/4 cup bread crumbs in a shallow dish and dredge the patties in bread crumbs.

Cook patties, in a little vegetable oil, on medium-high heat for about 4 minutes on each side or until browned.

SAUCE PREPARATION:

Mix the ingredients in a blender, and process until smooth. Add more water for a thinner sauce.

Serve with blended sauce and choice of fresh vegetables. I do like to serve these in a warmed pita.

Red-Lentil Mushroom Burger with Aioli

AIOLI INGREDIENTS:

1/4 cup veganaise

1 tsp fresh lemon juice

1 tsp fresh cilantro, chopped

1 garlic clove, minced

AIOLI DIRECTIONS:

Mix all together.

burger simplicity

BURGER INGREDIENTS:

2 cups water

3/4 cup dried red lentils

1/2 tsp salt

2 Tbsp olive oil

1 cup diced onion

1/2 cup finely diced carrot

3 garlic cloves, minced

2 cups mushrooms, chopped fine

1 tsp dried marjoram

1/4 tsp red pepper

3 Tbsp soy sauce

1/3 cup dry bread crumbs

1 Tbsp fresh lemon juice

2 Egg Replacer of ground flax and water

BURGER DIRECTIONS:

In a medium saucepan, combine water, lentils, and salt. Bring to a boil, cover, reduce heat to medium-low, and simmer 20 minutes. Drain and set aside to cool.

Sauté the onion, carrot, and garlic in olive oil for about 4 minutes. Add mushrooms, marjoram, and pepper. Cook for an additional 3 minutes, stirring occasionally. Add soy sauce and cook for another couple minutes or until liquid is almost evaporated. Place onion mixture in a large bowl and let cool for 5 minutes. Add the lentils, bread crumbs, lemon juice, and egg replacer. give it a little mix, and chill 30 minutes.

Stir lentil mix a bit and divide into 6 equal portions, shaping each portion into 1/2 inch patties. Cook over medium-high heat for about 5 minutes on each side.

Serve with aioli sauce and your favorite condiments.

Middle Eastern Potato Chickpea Burgers

INGREDIENTS:

1/2 lb. red potatoes, cooked and cooled

3 Tbsp olive oil, divided

1 tsp garlic, minced

1 - 15 oz. can garbanzo beans, rinsed

2 Tbsp chopped fresh parsley

1/2 tsp sea salt

1 Tbsp lemon zest

1 tsp smoked paprika

1/4 tsp freshly ground red pepper

2 egg replacer of ground flax seed and water

DIRECTIONS:

Place all ingredients into a food processor and pulse a few times until the mixture is easily formed and not falling apart. Form into 3/4-inch thick patties and cook over medium-high heat for about 3 to 5 minutes on each side.

side *simplicity*

side simplicity

It seems that we are always trying to complicate things and that's what keeps messing us up into the mentality that vegan cooking is complicated. What is so complicated about warming up some vegetables and putting them in a bowl? The simpler the side, the better!
In this world of complication, it is actually quite refreshing to see a simple wholesome item. You can take literally any vegetable, rice, pasta, or potato and make it taste great with a pinch of sea salt and pepper. If you want to go even farther with it add a little vegan butter spread, or an extremely light spice.

Quite honestly, when I go to a potluck or fellowship meal, the last thing I want is to wonder what strange things are in that side.

[*Plain and Simple*]
is the new "IN" in society.

side simplicity

[Vegetable Simplicity]

When we simplify our cooking processes, we are letting God's great food do all the work. We are not covering up His great flavors. One thing I like to do when it comes to sides, or any dish for that matter, is to give it that visual appeal. People eat more with their eyes than anything. If you have a side of green beans, add a little red pepper, almond slivers, or onion. This will not really complicate the flavor, but will certainly give it the wow factor on the visual appeal. Even a lemon wedge in the corner draws the eye to make it appetizing.

Look at these vegetable dishes that take no time whatsoever to produce. Whether you steam, simmer, or sauté; their simple fresh approach is the appeal that we want to attract our appetite.

side simplicity

[Rice Simplicity]

Rice is one of the easiest items to cook, especially with the invention of the rice cooker. When cooking rice, it all comes down to the science of ratios. How much water to how much rice? The general rule of thumb is 1 part rice to 2 parts water. If you want a sticky rice, add more water; and if you want a firmer rice, use less water.

Without a rice cooker, you will want to bring the water to a boil and then simmer for 20 minutes, or make it easy and get a rice cooker. Commercially, I used to put the water and rice into an insert and place it into a steam-table in the morning, and by noon it was ready to go.

Flavor wise, you can add flavor to the water before cooking, or wait until it is cooked and flavor a bit before serving. Just remember that when it comes to salt, it will take a lot of salt in the water to get the flavor you're looking for and most of it is going to be absorbed into the rice, adding excess salt into your diet. You are a lot better off doing the salting after the rice is cooked, health-wise, you will use a lot less.

When it comes to rice, we must again go to the presentation factor. If it looks appealing, it will attract the appetite. Adding color from minced vegetables, and spices will give each rice creation its own personality.

263

side simplicity

[Potato Simplicity]

Potatoes are one of the healthiest foods we can ever eat. I have heard it said that we could life perfectly healthy on a diet that consisted of exclusively potatoes and nothing else. They're healthy, they're relatively inexpensive, they're available year round, and they taste great, so eat them regularly.

I could write a whole book on the potato alone, but for today I will just look at the simplicity of the potato. There are any ways to prepare a potato, and in all reality, you could even eat them raw; but for the most part they are always cooked one way or another.

We touched base on the baking or broiling vegetables and the potato is no different when it comes to slicing a couple and tossing them in the oven. Whole baked potatoes are as easy as putting them in the oven at 350 for about 1 hour, depending on the size. Some people foil wrap the potatoes, while others will oil and salt them. It all depends what you're looking for. There are a hundred right ways to cook a potato, it just depends what you want to do with it.

Mashed potatoes are one of my favorite foods. I can make mashed potatoes in no time at all. All I have to do is put the drained, hot boiled potatoes in a mixer and add a couple ingredients like salt, and pepper, and they're ready to eat. To help in your flavors, adding nutmeg works really great, green onions are awesome and of course, the vegan butter. For the textures, when blending mashed potatoes, you can use water or even better is a little bit of soy milk. This will give it a better creamier feel, vegan sour cream can also be added.

I often use the potatoes with the skin on because it gives a more fresh natural appearance. It is called "country style" when you leave the skin on. It is also okay to leave the potatoes a little bit on the lumpy side, again portraying the natural look.

I can generally tell if a potato is an instant, or a real fresh whipped. Commercially, I would very often use the instant potatoes, and add a couple huge handfuls of boiled off, skin on, potatoes. People would never know the difference.

Boiled potatoes are also great for the refrigerator, because you can use them for a great number of items. Normally what I like to do with the boiled potatoes is drain them while they are still hot and then let them air dry for a couple of hours. This will dry a lot of the moisture out of the potato and tighten them up. Then I put them in the fridge for later use. They are now ready for hash-browns, potato salad, putting into soups, or even slicing and grilling. I almost always have a container of cooked off potatoes ready to eat. It is actually one of the ways to make your kitchen time so much easier.

There are also plenty of varieties of potatoes that you can do these simple techniques with. Russets are a favorite for baked, hash-browns and mashed, while baby reds do quite well for potato salads and soups. I also like the Yukon Gold potatoes for everything. Regardless of what potato you use, you are sure to eat more of them now that you know how to prepare them easier.

Vegan Crock-pot Stuffing

INGREDIENTS:

2 cups chopped onions

2 cups chopped celery

1/8 cup vegan margarine

1 cup mushrooms, sliced

1/4 cup chopped fresh parsley

1 Tbsp poultry seasoning

1 Tbsp sage

1 tsp dried thyme

1/2 tsp red pepper

1/2 tsp marjoram

4 cups veggie broth

12 cups dried out cornbread or bread, 1 inch tears (or use a combo of the two)

DIRECTIONS:

Sauté onions, celery, and mushrooms in margarine until onions are golden brown. Add liquid and spices and mix.

In a very large mixing bowl, pour liquid over breadcrumbs. Pour in enough broth to moisten. If dry, add a bit of water to moisten. Lightly pack stuffing into crock pot, and cover. Set on high for 45 minutes then reduce to low and cook for 3 to 4 hours. Makes about 8 to 10 servings.

entree
simplicity

entree simplicity

Dinners have traditionally been known as the largest meal of the day. Try to do more simple and lighter meals. These great light entrees can be flavored in a number of different ways. You can use sauces, pestos, or maybe just a little salt and pepper. Of course if your taste buds are vegan and not coated with grease, these dishes will taste great with nothing at all. Just remember that your last meal of the day is supposed to be your smallest, so keep your portion sizes to a minimum.

Spinach & Pesto Lasagna

Once you have the recipes of sauce, ricotta, and pesto, the rest is easy.

INGREDIENTS:

12 lasagna noodles, cooked

Mushroom sauce

Ricotta cheese

Pesto sauce

3 cups baby spinach, chopped

3 cups vegan mozzarella, shredded

MUSHROOM SAUCE INGREDIENTS:

3 Tbsp vegan margarine

3 shallots, minced

1/4 cup all purpose flour

2 1/2 cups almond milk

1/4 cup lemon juice

1/4 cup white grape juice

1/4 tsp salt

2 Tbsp vegan Parmesan cheese

1 lb. mushrooms, diced

DIRECTIONS:

Preheat oven to 350 degrees. You will also need to boil the noodles until al dente (firm, yet flexible). There are also some pre-cooked noodles if available.

Next we are going to lightly mix the pesto, ricotta and chopped spinach.

To Assemble: Spread a couple ladles full of sauce on the bottom of a 10×13" baking dish. Next, place 4 noodles on the bottom of the pan. Add about 6 tablespoons of the mixture onto each noodle then top with a little vegan cheese. Repeat this step until the pan is full. Cover with foil and bake for 40-45 minutes. For the last 10 minutes of baking, you can remove the foil and continue baking in order to melt the cheese on top. Let rest for a couple of minutes before cutting.

SAUCE DIRECTIONS:

In a large saucepan, melt the margarine over medium-high heat. Add the shallots and saute for a couple of minutes. Whisk in the flour. Add the almond milk and cook until it begins to thicken, stirring often. Add the remaining ingredients and it's ready to serve.

NOTE: You will also taste that this makes a great mushroom dip.

VEGAN RICOTTA CHEESE INGREDIENTS:

1 -14oz. pkg extra firm tofu, drained and pressed

1/3 cup nutritional yeast

1 cup fresh basil leaves

1 tsp garlic powder

1 tsp salt

1/4 tsp red pepper

2 Tbsp lemon juice

1/2 cup vegan mozzarella, shredded

RICOTTA CHEESE DIRECTIONS:

Combine all the ingredients, except the tofu and mozzarella cheese, in a food processor until smooth and then add the tofu and pulse a couple times until it has the texture of ricotta cheese. Transfer to a bowl. Stir in the cheese.

PESTO INGREDIENTS:

2 1/2 cups fresh basil leaves, chopped

1/2 cup parsley

1 cup pine nuts

4 cloves garlic, minced

1/4 tsp salt

1/8 tsp red pepper

1/8 cup lemon juice

1/3 cup olive oil

1/4 cup vegan Parmesan cheese

PESTO DIRECTIONS:

Combine all the ingredients in a food processor until choppy smooth (not over blended).

Lentil Crusted Faux Scallops

INGREDIENTS:

2 - 14 oz. packs tofu, firm

Salt & pepper to taste

1/2 cup dry lentils, ground into a flour using a spice grinder

1/2 cup all purpose unbleached flour

1 tsp paprika

1/2 tsp salt

Pinch of cayenne

Salt & pepper to taste

DIRECTIONS:

Preheat oven to 400 degrees. Using a cookie cutter, cut circles out of the tofu the size of scallops, you should get 4 or 5 out of each block of tofu. If the tofu is thick enough, you can get 8 to 10 pieces by cutting them in half

Use the remaining tofu and blend with a little soy milk to replace an egg wash.

You are going to bread the tofu by first placing them in a mixture of flour, salt, pepper and paprika. Then dredge into the soy milk mixture, and then into the ground lentil. Press crust mixture well onto the tofu and then carefully place into a very hot pan coated with a little olive oil.

Cook for about 3 minutes or until golden brown. Turn over tofu in pan and cook for another 3 minutes. Place tofu scallops, into oven and cook for about 5 minutes more or until the tofu is firm and browned. Remove and serve immediately.

Scallops are delicious by themselves or atop a vegetable medley of your choice. Garnish tofu with the tomato topping and a drizzle of curry oil.

entree simplicity

TOMATO TOPPING INGREDIENTS:

6 Roma tomatoes (peeled, cut in half lengthwise and seeded)

2 garlic cloves (very thinly slivered)

Salt to taste

DIRECTIONS:

Place tomatoes and garlic on a sheet pan and cook in a preheated 400 degree oven for about 20 minutes or until tomatoes are very soft. Set the tomatoes aside and reserve until needed.

CURRY OIL INGREDIENTS:

6 Tbsp corn oil

1/2 Tbsp curry powder

1/2 tsp minced shallot

1/2 tsp minced garlic

DIRECTIONS:

Heat a small pan over medium heat with one tablespoon of corn oil, then add the shallot and garlic, and sauté them for about two minutes. Add curry and toast for about 20 seconds. Add remaining oil, and then immediately remove from heat. Whisk well and let rest to allow the flavors to blend.

entree simplicity

Spinach Pesto Pasta and Grilled Zucchini

INGREDIENTS:

2 medium zucchini

4 cups cooked spinach spaghetti

1 cup spinach pesto

1 cup fresh spinach

1 lemon, zest and juice

2 cloves garlic, minced

SPINACH PESTO:

4 cups fresh spinach, lightly packed

1/3 cup fresh basil leaves, packed

1/3 cup fresh parsley leaves, packed

1/2 cup pine nuts

1/2 cup olive oil

1 lemon, zest and juice

2 Tbsp garlic, chopped

1/4 tsp sea salt

DIRECTIONS:

Slice zucchini into thick 1/2 inch slices. Char-broil or grill on high, just until half cooked.

Sauté all the ingredients together, reserving the spinach for the last minute right before serving. Remove the spaghetti and spiral into a mini tower and surround with the remaining product. You may want to do this in batches, or you can do all the spaghetti in one pan and the zucchini in another. Either way, it's simple and has a huge flavor impact that you will love.

DIRECTIONS FOR SPINACH PESTO:

Blend all ingredients well in a food processor.

People who quit will *never know* how close they really were to success.
-Mark Anthony

stuffing stuff
simplicity

There is nothing easier than getting a great presentation by simply stuffing stuff. It is a visual effect that will enhance any meal. Fast and easy, and the things we can stuff are endless. Both what we stuff and what we stuff them with are equally limited only by your imagination.

Here are some great stuffing ideas and I am sure that the picture is worth ten thousand words.

stuffing stuff simplicity

[*Stuffed Tomatoes*]

Tomato stuffing is a simple culinary technique that can WOW anybody. You can stuff tomatoes with hundreds of different items and you can also do different cuts to the tomatoes to get an even greater visual appeal.

These tomatoes can also be served cold or baked. One suggestion that if you are going to do a baked stuffed tomato, a smooth cut top works the best. I like to cook the stuffing first and then fill the tomato and finish it off in the oven for just a few minutes. This way the tomato will not be over cooked with a cold centered stuffing.

Stuffed Cabbage Roll Simplicity

There is something special about an entree of stuffed cabbage rolls. They always seem to present a feeling of love. It must be the savory aromas and the visual thoughts of care in rolling up each cabbage that draws us to the surprise of delectable awaiting flavors. Most people think that it is a time consuming complicated creation way beyond anyone's abilities, when in reality they are extremely easy to make.

I do want to give you a couple tips that will make your cabbage roll recipes easier than you could ever imagine.

The first thing is the cabbage and we want to make our job easy. The easiest way to do the cabbage is to peel off the leaves of a cabbage and put them boiling water for 5 minutes and then drain and rinse with cold water. All we really want to do is soften them enough to roll easily.

No need for salt in the boiling water and don't put the whole cabbage in the water, like many recipes tell you to do. All that does is make it so the leaves are not evenly cooked and difficult to peel in one piece. You can use green or red cabbage, and other great rollings are the grape leaf, large kale, swiss chard, and even collard greens.

stuffing stuff simplicity

And the greatest part about cabbage rolls is that you can fill them with pretty much anything. The popularity is generally rice, even though we can go to the beyond with potatoes, corn meals, vegetable blends, and a wide variety of fillings. The trick is to keep a filling that is not too dry and not too wet.   When it comes to rice, keep in mind that it is going to expand a little when you are baking them, so you really don't want to wrap them extremely tight. I also like to have a rice that is on the stickier side because it will bind together without the addition of eggs, like many recipes use.

As far as sauces go, there is always the traditional tomato sauce, but I would suggest diving into brown and white sauces. Let's jump into the beyond with a salsa or green chili. If you want to go steps even farther into the wow factor, try an Asian sweet and sour, or teriyaki. What about a pesto,or garlic lemon-lime?

Fast, easy, and definitely producing a wow factor. What else can you ask for in a meal? Well how about the healthy side? Yes it's an extremely healthy meal too!

[Beyond Directions]

COOKING THE RICE:

Generally the ratio will be one part rice and two parts water. I like to cook the rice as a one step process by adding all the vegetables, peppers, onions, and spices to the same pot. There is really no reason to take the extra steps of dirtying up a bunch of other pots. You can sauté some onions, to a dark brown flavor, which is really great for cabbage rolls.

Place all the ingredients into a pot, and bring to a boil. Reduce heat to low, cover, and simmer 40 minutes, until tender.

Add any additional ingredients like textured vegetable protein, nuts, craisins, or whole beans. Stir in well and your stuffing is ready to go. I will often stir in a little tomato sauce, or juice for a flavor blast and get the rice to a consistency that I'm looking for.

COOKING THE CABBAGE:

It only takes about 5 minutes in boiling water. You can add flavor to the water, but it's really not necessary. I do put the leaves in the pot separately and not the whole cabbage, this will make your product much more consistent and easier to handle. Just core out the cabbage and peel the outer leaves. I will use the inside cabbage for salads.

Drain the cabbage and run cold water over the leaves. This will help the leaves have a more vibrant color. The leaves should be flexible enough to roll, but not overcooked to be falling apart. Once they're cool and drained, they are ready to be stuffed.

FILLING THE CABBAGE:

Now that the rice is a little cooler and the cabbage is cooled down, they are ready to stuff. We are going to start at the rib, or thick side of the cabbage, and place a couple heaping tablespoons of filling as desired size. We are going to roll the cabbage, like a burrito, folding in the sides as we go. At the end, the thinner part of the leaf should be the last fold.

SAUCE TOPPING:

The sauce can go in a thousand directions. I try to have sauces that I can just mix and pour over the top without needing to cook them. This makes your job easier.

BAKING THE CABBAGE ROLLS:

I like to lace the bottom of the pan with sauce before placing the cabbage rolls in the pan. If you want to spray the pans to help clean up that's fine too.

When placing the cabbage rolls into the pan, we want to place the last fold to the bottom of the pan, this will help the sealing. Cover the cabbage with the remaining sauce and ingredients and then bake in the oven, covered, for about 30 to 60 minutes at 350 degrees. You can always remove the cover and return to the oven for the last 10 minutes to brown the top if you like.

It's really that easy, and everyone will love them.

stuffing stuff simplicity

Basic Stuffed Cabbage Rolls Recipe

INGREDIENTS:

Cabbage

1 head green cabbage, leaves only

ADD IN ITEMS:

2 cups textured vegetable protein, pre soaked

1/2 cup slivered almonds

FILLING TO COOK:

1 cup rice

2 cups water

1 onion, fine diced

1/2 carrot, fine diced

1/2 red bell pepper, diced

3 cloves garlic, minced

1/2 tsp chili powder

1 tsp salt

SAUCE MIX:

2 - 10 oz. cans tomato soup

1 can diced stewed tomatoes

1 Tbsp dried basil

1 Tbsp dried oregano

Savory Vegetable Stuffed Cabbage

INGREDIENTS:

Green cabbage leaves, steamed until tender, but not falling apart

FILLING:

2 cups cooked rice

3 Tbsp vegan margarine

1 medium onion, diced

1 bell pepper diced, red or yellow

2 ribs celery, chopped fine

4 cloves of garlic, minced or pressed

1/4 tsp salt

SAUCE:

1 - 14.5oz. can tomato sauce

2 cups vegetable stock

½ Tbsp oregano

1/2 tsp thyme

1/2 tsp basil

stuffing stuff simplicity

Bean Stuffed Cabbage Rolls

INGREDIENTS:

Green cabbage leaves, steamed until tender, but not falling apart

FILLING:

1 cup brown rice, cooked

1 - 16 oz. can white beans, rinsed slightly mashed

1 cup onion, finely diced

1 tsp oregano

1/2 tsp dried basil

1/4 tsp salt

1/4 tsp pepper

SAUCE:

12 oz. tomato sauce

6 oz. tomato paste

1 cup vegetable stock

1 cup onion, finely chopped

2 cloves garlic, crushed

2 tsp natural sugar

1 tsp oregano

1/2 tsp basil

1/4 tsp pepper

Middle Eastern Cabbage Rolls

FILLING TO COOK:

1 cup basmati rice

1 cup lentils

5 cups water

1 onion, diced

1 red bell pepper, diced

3 cloves garlic, minced

1/4 tsp turmeric

1/4 tsp curry

1/2 tsp salt

1/4 tsp red pepper

ADD IN ITEMS:

3/4 cup raisins

3/4 cup toasted almonds, coarsely chopped

SAUCE:

3 - 28 oz. cans stewed tomatoes

1/4 cup lemon juice

1/4 cup cilantro, fresh chopped

4 tsp dried basil

1 Tbsp ground cinnamon

1 tsp nutmeg

1 tsp cardamon

1/2 tsp salt

1/2 tsp red pepper

Polish Stuffed Cabbage Rolls

INGREDIENTS:

2 large cabbages, with big leaves, core removed

FILLING TO COOK:

2 cups long grain rice

4 cups water

1/4 cup vegan margarine

1 large onion, diced

2 lb. mushrooms, chopped

3 Tbsp Worcestershire sauce

2 Tbsp garlic, minced

2 Tbsp paprika

1 tsp salt

1 tsp red pepper

SAUCE:

6 cups tomato sauce

1/4 cup paprika

1/4 cup fresh chopped parsley

2 Tbsp garlic

1 Tbsp onion powder

1/2 tsp chili powder

1/4 tsp cumin

Greek Stuffed Cabbage Rolls

INGREDIENTS:

30 cabbage leaves or chard

FOR THE FILLING:

2 cups long grain rice, overcooked

1 large onion, finely chopped

3 ripe medium tomatoes, finely chopped

1/4 cup dill

2 Tbsp olive oil

FOR THE SAUCE:

2/3 cup finely chopped zucchini or Italian squash

1 cup vegetable stock

1/2 cup fresh parsley, fine chopped

1/2 cup fresh mint, fine chopped

1/2 tsp pepper

1 tsp cumin

DIRECTIONS:

Bring to a boil, thicken with slurry, or roux. Cover cabbage rolls and bake at 350 degrees, covered for 40 minutes. Drizzle with Cucumber Sauce.

dessert simplicity

dessert simplicity

[Fruit Simplicity]

One of my favorite desserts is to just have some fruit. Far too often we eat a healthy meal, only to top it off with a sugary, high calorie, high fat dessert. Sometimes the best desserts are the simplest ones. Here are some desserts that really need no recipe and yet have a far better attraction than the high fat and sugar desserts.

dessert simplicity

[Parfait Simplicity]

Once again the greatest desserts are the simplest ones. Parfaits are very easy to produce when you have the right ingredients on hand. Granola should already be a staple in your home as well as the fresh fruits. Beyond that, I always have some pie filling because it is so easy to whip into a quick dessert. And speaking of whipping, there are great vegan whip toppings out there, one of which is the "SoyaToo" that can be whipped with a hand mixer in 3 minutes and has great stability in the fridge.

So with all these great foods that God has provided, there is no reason to purchase the processed foods that man has concocted.

dessert simplicity

[Ice Cream Simplicity]

Ice cream is now available in all vegan forms and I am now seeing them in more general food stores. Just don't be fooled by the lactose free, or dairy free labeling because many of those still have animal products like whey. I even found one that the first ingredients were milk, sugar, and cream. So make sure to read those labels. You will find a lot of soy and rice milk ice creams, but the favorite one I have found is the coconut milk ice cream. These ice creams may seem a little more expensive, but the price has really dropped over the years, and portion for portion, it is still a less expensive option than most desserts. You can also make your own and save even more money.

BALSAMIC VINEGAR & ICE CREAM

The next time you really want to blow your guests away with the most awesome dessert, give them a couple scoops of your favorite vegan vanilla ice cream, and then top it with a heavy splash of 18 year old balsamic vinegar. It is the simplest ice cream dessert you will ever find and your guests will have a great WOW of surprise.

dessert simplicity

Banana Ice Cream

INGREDIENTS:

Bananas, frozen solid

Soy milk

Sweetener

DIRECTIONS:

Use one or more frozen bananas per serving. If the bananas are not sliced, break them into pieces and put them into your food processor or high powered blenders work best. Begin processing, and slowly drizzle in soy milk until it is the consistency of ice cream. Add sweetener like agave, or natural sugar if desired, and it doesn't take a lot, just a teaspoon or less per banana. You can add flavor like vanilla too. You might need to stop and give the bananas a little stir with a spoon, but they will soon blend on their own, just be careful not to put too much milk in them. Blend and serve.

VARIATIONS: Add cocoa powder while processing to create chocolate-banana ice cream; add walnuts for banana-walnut "ice cream"

NOTE: Other frozen fruits work well, too. Try peaches, mangos, strawberries, or any combinations.

Pineapple Sorbet Simplicity

INGREDIENTS:

Any canned pineapple chunks packed in juice.

DIRECTIONS:

Take the pineapple, juice and all, and freeze in a freezer safe container. Break up the frozen fruit a bit and put into a food processor or preferred high powered blender and blend until smooth and creamy. This may take a couple minutes and you may need to give it a hand mix a couple times through the process, but it will soon be blending on its own. It's ready to serve. And yeah, it's really that simple. You can add a little sweetener if you like, or what I like to do is fold in some fresh blueberries right before serving. Even top with a vegan whip topping and coconut flakes. A little coconut milk helps the blending and gives it a little added flavor too.

[Fruit Crisp Simplicity]

It is real easy to make a vegan crisp when you have the right products. All you have to do is take a baking dish and put a couple cans of fruit pie filling in it. Top it with about 2 cups of any vegan white cake mix and a good splashing of melted vegan margarine. Bake at 350 degrees for about 20 to 30 minutes or until golden brown.

The filling does not need to be store bought. You can always make your own by boiling fruit and thickening it with cornstarch. It is often less expensive this way and you don't need to have near as much sugar as the store bought brands. Sliced apples for example can be boiled in water with a little cinnamon, and brown sugar; then thickened with a corn starch and water slurry. Peach crisp, berry crisp, cherry crisp - the list goes on.

As for the toppings, the white cake mix is easy and cost effective. But you can also run with a topping of oatmeal, or blend a flour sugar salt combination. For a little added touch, top with raisins, nuts, or coconut. Whatever crisp sensations you create, you're bound to enjoy the simplicity of these fast and easy desserts.

Crock-pot Pumpkin Pie

INGREDIENTS:

4 cups cubed white bread

3 cups vanilla soy milk

1 - 16-ounce can solid-pack pumpkin

3/4 cup firmly packed light brown sugar

1/4 cup apple juice

2 tsp pure vanilla extract

2 tsp ground cinnamon

1/2 tsp ground ginger

1/4 tsp ground allspice

1/4 tsp ground nutmeg

1/4 tsp salt

DIRECTIONS:

Press half the bread cubes into the bottom of a lightly oiled 4-quart slow cooker. In a medium-size saucepan, heat the soy milk until hot, but do not let it come to a boil. Remove the pan from the heat and set aside.

In a large mixing bowl, combine the pumpkin, brown sugar, apple juice, vanilla, spices, and salt.

Blend well, then slowly add the hot milk, stirring constantly. Carefully pour half the pumpkin mixture over the bread and push the bread pieces down beneath the mixture to moisten them. Repeat with remaining bread and pumpkin mixture. Cover and cook on low for 3 hours, until firm. Turn off the slow cooker and let the pudding sit, covered, for 20 minutes before serving.

Serves: 6 to 8

Vegan Pumpkin Pie

INGREDIENTS:

2 cups solid-pack canned pumpkin

1 cup soy milk

3/4 c. brown sugar

1/4 c. cornstarch

1 Tbsp molasses

1 tsp ground cinnamon

1 tsp pumpkin pie spice or 1/2 tsp nutmeg

1 tsp vanilla

DIRECTIONS:

Preheat oven to 350 degrees. Blend all ingredients extremely well in a blender. Pour into a 9" unbaked pastry crust and cook for about 50 minutes or until firm on the edges. Center may be a little jiggly, but will set up when placed in the fridge overnight.

Peach Cobbler Cake

INGREDIENTS:

3/4 cup flour, (all or part whole wheat)

1/4 cup soy flour

2 tsp baking powder

1/2 tsp cinnamon

1/2 tsp nutmeg

1/2 cup sugar

2/3 cup soy milk

1/4 tsp almond extract

1 - 16-ounce can sliced peaches, well drained & cut into 1/2" pieces

DIRECTIONS:

Preheat the oven to 350 degrees. In a medium bowl combine the flours, baking powder, cinnamon, nutmeg and sugar. Stir together well.

Add soy milk and almond extract and stir just until blended. Gently stir in the well-drained and chopped peaches.

Pour the batter into an 8" square baking pan coated with nonstick spray. Bake at 350 degrees for 35-40 minutes, until a toothpick inserted in the center comes out clean. Cut into 9 squares to serve.

dessert simplicity

Fat-Free Lemon Pie

INGREDIENTS:

1 1/2 cups natural sugar

1/2 cup cornstarch

1/4 tsp salt

1 1/4 cups water

1 cup soy milk

3/4 cup lemon juice

Zest of 2 lemons

DIRECTIONS:

Combine sugar, cornstarch, and salt in saucepan, stir in water and soy milk. Bring to a boil and simmer for about 4 minutes, stirring constantly until thick. Remove from heat and slowly add the lemon juice and zest. You are determining the body of your pie by how much juice you put in the product, too much will give you a loose filling, too little juice will give you a tight filling. You may want a different thickness based on what you are going to do with it. Either way, it will taste great. You will get the feel of this after you do it once. Pour into a pie crust or graham cracker crust and chill.

dessert simplicity

Oil Free Pumpkin Bread

INGREDIENTS:

1 1/2 cups sugar

1 cup canned pumpkin

1/2 cup applesauce

1/2 cup water

Egg replacer for 3 eggs

1 2/3 cups flour

1 tsp soda

1 tsp cinnamon

3/4 tsp salt

1/2 tsp baking powder

1/2 tsp nutmeg

1/4 tsp cloves

1/4 cup walnuts or pecans, chopped fine

DIRECTIONS:

For your wet mix. Combine first five ingredients in a small bowl and beat well. In a separate bowl, combine remaining ingredients for your dry mix. Gradually mix the two together, stir in nuts.
Pour batter into a lightly coated 9"x 5" loaf pan and bake at 350 degrees for 65 to 70 minutes or until toothpick inserted in the middle comes out clean. Allow to cool 10 minutes in the pan before removing.

Vegan Eggnog Cheesecake

INGREDIENTS:

1 - 12oz. package extra firm light silken tofu, drained

1 - 8-ounce package Tofutti cream cheese

3/4 cup natural sugar

1/2 cup vegan eggnog or vanilla soy milk

2 Tbsp lemon juice

3 Tbsp rum extract

1 tsp vanilla

1 tsp ground nutmeg

3 Tbsp cornstarch

1 prepared graham cracker or oatmeal cookie crust

DIRECTIONS:

Preheat oven to 350 degrees. Blend cream cheese and tofu in a food processor until smooth. Add the sugar and milk, and process for a good 3 minutes. Add the remaining ingredients and process until completely smooth, about 3 more minutes. Pour into the pie crust and bake in the oven for about 55 minutes. Filling will be slightly jiggly and not completely set until chilled, just try not to have a browned top.

Remove from oven and cool. Refrigerate overnight, serve sprinkled with additional grated nutmeg

dessert simplicity

Pumpkin Leather Roll-Ups

INGREDIENTS:

1 cup canned pumpkin pie filling

1 cup unsweetened applesauce

DIRECTIONS:

Line an extra large baking sheet pan with plastic wrap and spray lightly with pan spray. In medium bowl, combine pumpkin pie mix and applesauce. Spread mixture evenly over bottom of pan; smooth with spatula to an extremely thin layer. The thinner the layer the quicker the cook. Dry in 140 degree oven for 8 to 10 hours, until surface is no longer sticky to the touch. Remove from oven; cool slightly. Peel back slowly off the saran wrap. Cut into desired lengths. Roll up and wrap tightly in plastic wrap.

Beet Cake with Peanut Butter -N- Banana Sauce

INGREDIENTS:

Wet Mix

1 cup beets, drained and pureed

1 cup applesauce

1 Tbsp vanilla extract

1 tsp apple cider vinegar

1/2 cup agave nectar

Dry Mix

1 cup whole wheat flour

1/2 cup unbleached white flour

1/2 cup cocoa or carob powder

1 cup natural sugar

1 Tbsp cornstarch

2 tsp baking soda

1/2 tsp salt

1/4 tsp cinnamon

DIRECTIONS:

Preheat the oven to 325 degrees. Take the wet ingredients and mix well. Mix the dry ingredients together and then add them beet mixture and stir until well-combined. Pour into a 9"x11", lightly oiled baking pan and bake for about 35 minutes. Test by inserting a toothpick into the center; it's done when the toothpick comes out clean. Allow to cool completely before cutting and serving.

Banana-Peanut Butter Sauce

INGREDIENTS:

6 oz. firm silken tofu

1 banana

2 Tbsp natural peanut butter

1/3 cup agave nectar, to taste

1/2 tsp vanilla

1/4 tsp lemon juice

DIRECTIONS:

Blend all ingredients in a food processor until smooth. Refrigerate until needed. The sauce can thicken in the fridge, so it's best to give it time to chill. Serve over cake. Makes 8 servings.

Bake for about 30 minutes, until the top is golden browned. Allow to cool before cutting into bars. Number of servings (yield): 16

Double-Layer Pumpkin Cheesecake

FIRST MIX INGREDIENTS:

1 - 8 oz. Tofutti cream cheese

12 oz. tofu, light firm or extra firm silken

1/2 cup natural sugar

2 Tbsp cornstarch

1 1/2 Tbsp lemon juice

1 tsp vanilla

ADD IN INGREDIENTS:

1/2 cup pumpkin puree, canned

2 tsp rum extract

3 Tbsp brown sugar

1/2 tsp cinnamon

1/4 tsp ginger

1/4 tsp grated fresh nutmeg

1 pre-made 8-inch graham cracker crust

DIRECTIONS:

Preheat the oven to 375 degrees. Put the first set of ingredients in a food processor and puree until completely and extremely smooth. Set aside a heaping cup of this mixture to spread on the top.

Add the next set of ingredients to the remaining mixture in the food processor and process until well blended. Smooth it carefully in the crust, then top with the reserved portion and make sure it is a little heaping in the middle. Bake until the center is almost set, about 50-60 minutes. (Insert a toothpick. If it comes out wet and cold, give it more time, until the center is firm.) Remove from the oven and allow to cool. Refrigerate until completely chilled, at least 3 hours, and serve.

Serves 8.

dessert simplicity

Chocolate a l'Orange Mousse Pie

INGREDIENTS:

1 - 12oz. package tofu, silken firm

10 oz. semi-sweet chocolate chips, or carob

1 Tbsp orange extract

2 Tbsp orange zest

1 Tbsp maple syrup

Prepared graham cracker crust

Sliced almonds and grated orange peel for garnish

DIRECTIONS:

Blend tofu, orange extract, and maple syrup in food processor or blender until smooth. Melt chocolate chips over double boiler. Put chocolate into processor and mix with tofu until creamy. Pour into a graham cracker crust and chill. Top with sliced almonds and orange peel. Serves 8

Blueberry-Oat Bars

FILLING INGREDIENTS:

1 pint blueberries

1/4 cup agave nectar

1/4 cup apple juice

1/2 tsp vanilla

2 Tbsp cornstarch mixed with 2 Tbsp water to form a slurry paste

CRUST INGREDIENTS:

3 cups oatmeal (regular, not instant)

1/2 tsp cinnamon

1 1/2 tsp baking powder

1/4 tsp salt

1/2 cup applesauce

6 Tbsp (3/8 cup) agave nectar

6 Tbsp (3/8 cup) water

1 tsp vanilla

DIRECTIONS:

Preheat oven to 375F. In a small saucepan, combine the blueberries, agave nectar, and juice. Bring to a boil over medium-high heat. When it boils, stir in the vanilla and cornstarch mixture. Continue to stir as the mixture thickens. Remove from heat and set aside.

Put 1/2 of the oatmeal into a blender and grind it to a fine powder. Pour it into a mixing bowl and add the remaining oatmeal, cinnamon, baking powder, and salt. Mix well, then stir in the apple sauce, agave nectar, water, and vanilla, and mix well. Spread half of the batter into a lightly oiled 8"×8" baking dish, smoothing well to cover the bottom of the pan. Spoon the blueberry filling over the batter, and then cover the blueberries with the remaining batter. Bake for 30 minutes or until golden.

NOTE: You can add a sugar glaze on top by mixing a little powdered sugar and water into a drizzling sauce. Gluten free oats, will produce a gluten free product.

dessert simplicity

Fat Free B.O.M. Cookies
Banana-Oat-Maple Cookies

INGREDIENTS:

Dry Mix

1 cup quick oats

1 cup white whole wheat flour

1/2 tsp baking soda

1/2 tsp baking powder

1/2 tsp salt

1 tsp cinnamon

1/4 cup raisins

Wet Mix

1 Tbsp banana extract

1/2 tsp vanilla

1/2 cup maple syrup

1 banana, mashed

1/2 tsp lemon juice

3 tsp ground flaxseed with 3 Tbsp water

DIRECTIONS:

Preheat the oven to 375 degrees. Mix the egg replacer of flaxseed and water and set aside.

Mix the oats, flour, baking soda, baking powder, salt, and cinnamon in a medium mixing bowl and add the raisins.

In another bowl, mix the wet ingredients and then mix in the flax-egg replacer. Pour into the dry mixture and stir well but don't over mix.

Drop heaping tablespoons onto a baking sheet lined with parchment paper. Flatten each cookie slightly with a fork. Bake for about 8-12 minutes or until bottoms and sides are lightly brown. Undercooking is best, they will cook a little as they cool. Makes about 15 cookies.

Low-Fat Peanut Butter Banana Cookies

INGREDIENTS:

Dry Mix

1 cup unbleached flour

1/2 cup whole wheat pastry flour

1 tsp baking powder

1 pinch salt

Wet Mix

1/2 cup natural peanut butter, chunky or smooth

1/4 cup brown sugar

1/2 cup sugar

3/4 cup mashed banana

1/4 cup chocolate chips or carob

DIRECTIONS:

Preheat oven to 375 degrees. Mix the dry items together, and in a separate container, mix the wet ingredients together. Then combine the two mixtures. Drop tablespoons full onto parchment lined sheet pans, about 2 inches apart. Flatten with a fork dipped in water. These cookies will not spread, so the shape they're in when they go into the oven will be about the same as when they come out. Bake for about 10 minutes, until bottoms are light brown. Makes about 20 cookies.

dessert simplicity

Gluten-Soy Free Cheese Cake

INGREDIENTS:

1 cup millet

4 cups water

1 tsp sea salt

1 tsp almond extract

2/3 cup cashews

2/3 cup lemon juice

2/3 cup maple syrup

DIRECTIONS:

Cook millet in 4 cups of water until water is absorbed but millet is not yet dry, about 40-50 minutes. Cool and blend with remaining ingredients in a food processor until very smooth. It's thick, and takes a little time. Pour into a pie plate and refrigerate. Top with fruit topping to serve.

FRUIT TOPPING:

12 oz. apple juice concentrate (not diluted)

4 Tbsp cornstarch mixed with 2 Tbsp of water

16 oz. fresh or frozen berries

DIRECTIONS:

Stir cornstarch mixture into apple concentrate and bring to a boil, stirring until thickened. Add berries and heat through. Chill and pour over cooled cheesecake.

Carob Chip Cookies

INGREDIENTS:

Wet Mix

1 cup water

1 cup walnuts (or raw cashews)

1/2 cup dates

1/2 tsp salt

2 tsp vanilla

Dry Mix

3/4 cups whole wheat flour

1/2 cup unbleached white flour

1 cup carob chips

1 cup raisins

DIRECTIONS:

Preheat oven to 350 degrees. Blend wet ingredients well in a blender. Stir in remaining ingredients. Drop by tablespoons on parchment paper lined baking sheet for about 20 to 25 minutes or until light brown.

dessert simplicity

Banana-Coconut Bars

INGREDIENTS:

Wet Mix

1/4 cup silken tofu, light or regular

3/4 cup brown sugar

1/4 cup vegan margarine

1/2 Tbsp vanilla extract

1 tsp rum extract

3 bananas, mashed

Dry Mix

1 1/2 cups unbleached flour

1 1/2 tsp baking powder

1 tsp salt

1/2 cup coconut flakes

DIRECTIONS:

Preheat oven to 350 degrees and lightly oil a 13"×9" inch baking dish. In a food processor, blend the tofu, margarine and sugar until smooth. Add the vanilla, rum extract, and mashed bananas, and stir well. Mix the dry ingredients and then we are going to combine the two mixes together. Stir just enough to moisten the flour, over-stirring makes them tough. Pour into the baking dish and put into the oven. Bake for 25-30 minutes, until an inserted toothpick comes out dry. Remove from the oven and while warm, not hot, cut into bars. Sprinkle with powdered sugar. Makes 12 bars.

dessert simplicity

Zucchini Muffins with Cinnamon-Crumb Topping

INGREDIENTS:

DRY MIX

2 cups white whole wheat flour
2 tsp baking powder
1 tsp baking soda
1/4 tsp salt
1/4 tsp nutmeg
1/2 cup natural sugar
1/4 cup raisins
1/4 cup chopped walnuts

WET MIX

Egg replacer 3 Tbsp water with 3 tsp ground flaxseed
1 1/4 cup shredded zucchini, packed
1 Tbsp lemon zest
1 Tbsp lemon juice
1 Tbsp agave nectar (or other liquid sweetener)
1 cup soy milk
1/2 cup apple sauce

CINNAMON CRUMB TOPPING

1 Tbsp margarine
2 Tbsp brown sugar
2 Tbsp flour
1/2 Tbsp cinnamon

DIRECTIONS:

Preheat oven to 400 degrees. Line a muffin pan with paper or spray well with non-stick spray. Mix all the dry ingredients. In a separate bowl, whisk the egg/flax replacer with the water. Add the remaining wet ingredients and mix. Combine the wet with the dry and stir just until moistened. Do not over-stir. Spoon into muffin cups. Mix the topping ingredients well with a fork until crumbly, and sprinkle the center of each muffin with a little topping. Bake until a toothpick comes out clean, about 20 minutes. Makes 12 muffins.

Fat-Free Pumpkin Cookies

INGREDIENTS:

DRY MIX

1/2 cup whole wheat flour

1/2 cup unbleached flour

1/4 cup rolled oats

1/2 tsp baking soda

1 tsp cinnamon

1/2 tsp ginger

1/2 tsp nutmeg

1/4 tsp salt

WET MIX

1/2 cup agave nectar

1/2 cup canned pumpkin

8 oz. firm tofu, blended until smooth

1 Tbsp vanilla extract

TOPPING

1 Tbsp natural sugar

DIRECTIONS:

Preheat oven to 375 degrees. Mix the dry ingredients together. In another bowl, mix the wet ingredients together. Add the wet ingredients to the dry and stir just until well-blended. Do not over-stir.

Drop rounded tablespoons of dough at least two inches apart on a parchment paper lined baking sheet. Flatten each cookie slightly with a fork. Sprinkle with natural sugar. Bake for 10-15 minutes or until edges are light and middle seem done. Remove from oven and allow to cool. Makes about 15 cookies.

dessert simplicity

Simple No Cook Icing

INGREDIENTS:

1 cup confectioner's sugar

2 tsp agave nectar

2 tsp non-dairy milk

1/8 tsp vanilla extract or any extract

Any food coloring, drop

DIRECTIONS:

Mix all the ingredients together. If it is too runny, add a little more sugar to balance it out. Spread over cooled cookies and allow to dry.

Sweet and Spicy Glazed Cashews

INGREDIENTS:

3 cups unsalted cashews, roasted or unroasted

3/4 cup white sugar

1/2 tsp dried crushed chili

1/2 tsp cayenne pepper

1/4 tsp salt

2 Tbsp vegetable oil

DIRECTIONS:

Spread cashews out on a baking sheet and place in the oven at 350 degrees. Allow to bake until cashews appear golden brown in color, about 15-30 minutes. If your cashews are already roasted, allow to bake for 10 minutes. Remove from oven and allow to cool slightly. Place a wok or large frying pan over medium-high heat. Add the oil, chili flakes and cayenne pepper. When oil is hot, add the nuts. Stir-fry until nuts are coated with chili oil, about 30 seconds. Add the salt and sugar and stir-fry for about 1 minute, or until the sugar has dissolved. Don't over-cook, or the sugar will start to burn.
Remove from heat. Slide nuts onto a sheet of parchment paper, or tin foil and allow to cool.

NOTE: Any type of nuts work too, such as pecans and walnuts.

extra
extra

3ABN COOKING PROGRAM RECIPES

HERE ARE RECIPES FROM MY LATEST 3ABN COOKING PROGRAMS

[Holiday Show "Family Traditions"]

Red Basil Mocktail

-By Mark Anthony

INGREDIENTS:

- 2 large leaves of basil or 1 tsp powdered basil per 12 oz. drink
- 1 part beet juice
- 1 part pineapple juice
- 1 part apple juice
- 3 parts tangerine

DIRECTIONS:

Blend vigorously until basil is totally incorporated and pour over ice. Garnish with fresh basil.

This drink is rich with many health benefits. The basil has magnesium, which helps lower your blood pressure. Tangerine is full of vitamin C. Pineapple juice contains bromelain, a protein-digesting enzyme that reduces inflammation. Apple juice can improve lung function. And the beet juice provides powerful antioxidant protection thanks to a vital nutrient called betacyanin.

Raspberry Cranberry Sauce

-By Melody Prettyman

INGREDIENTS:

1 lb. bag fresh cranberries, rinsed

1 can frozen 100% raspberry white grape juice

1 Tbsp lemon juice

1/4 cup Florida cane crystals, optional

1 tsp arrowroot powder

1/4 cup water

DIRECTIONS:

In a medium sauce pan add; cranberries, frozen juice, lemon juice and cane crystals. Bring to simmer and cook according to directions on cranberry package. When cranberries are done add arrowroot powder to water, stir and pour into cranberry mixture, stirring continuously for 3-5 minutes. Remove from heat and let set. Serve warm or chilled.

NOTE: You can also turn this into a great salad dressing by just thinning it down with orange juice.

Green Bean Casserole, Vegan Style

-By Melody Prettyman

INGREDIENTS:

4 cans green beans, drained

1-2 cups prepared mushroom soup

1 cup toasted onion rings

MUSHROOM SOUP:

3/4 cup raw cashews, rinsed

1/4 cup arrowroot powder or cornstarch

2 Tbsp onion powder

1 Tbsp salt, or to taste

2 Tbsp olive oil

1 lb. fresh mushrooms, diced fine

1 medium onion, diced fine

4 cups water

SOUP DIRECTIONS:

In a blender add; cashews, arrowroot powder, onion powder, salt and 2 cups water. Blend on high speed until smooth, about 5 minutes. In a sauce pan sauté olive oil, onions and mushrooms until tender. Reduce heat to medium low, pour blended cashew mixture over the sautéed mushroom mixture, add the remaining water and stir with a wire whisk until thickened. If you want a mushroom sauce for a casserole; add the additional water to the mushroom mixture ½- cup at a time until desired thickness.

CASSEROLE DIRECTIONS:

Preheat oven to 350 degrees. In a sprayed casserole dish add green beans and mushroom soup, mix until combined. Sprinkle toasted onion rings on top and bake in oven for 20-30 minutes or until golden brown. Serve warm.

Bird's Nests

-By Mark Anthony

INGREDIENTS:

2 extra large russet potatoes

1/4 cup cornstarch

4 cups vegetable oil for frying

Salt to taste

DIRECTIONS:

Shred raw potatoes and rinse with cold water, dust with cornstarch, form with appropriate deep frying baskets. Deep fry at 350 degrees for about 3 minutes, until golden brown. Salt to taste.

extra extra

Stuffing
-By Melody Prettyman

INGREDIENTS:

4-5 stalks celery, diced fine

1 large onion, diced fine

1 lb. bread of choice

2 Tbsp sage

1 Tbsp poultry seasoning

1 Tbsp McKay's chicken style seasoning

1 cup Leahey chicken style gravy mix

3 cups water

Salt to taste

DIRECTIONS:

In a large deep skillet add, celery, onions, McKay's chicken style seasoning and ½ cup water, simmer until vegetables are tender. Add gravy mix to remaining water, stir and add to the pan, simmer for 2-3 minutes or until mixture becomes thick. Mix to moisten all of the bread, remove pan from heat and cover. Let set for 15-20 minutes until all liquid is absorbed. Place stuffing mix into casserole dish and bake at 350 degrees for 15-20 minutes, or until top is golden brown. Remove and serve with cranberry raspberry sauce.

Totally Awesome Turkey Loaf

-By Melody Prettyman

INGREDIENTS:

3 cups water

1/8 cup onion powder

2 Tbsp olive oil, divided

1/8 cup McKay's chicken style seasoning, vegan special

1 Tbsp poultry seasoning

1 tsp garlic powder

1 tsp Bakon hickory style seasoning

1 tsp salt, or to taste

1 cup Leahey chicken style gravy powder, gluten-free

4 cups Butler soy curls

2 cups oats

1/4 cup flaxseed, ground

Parchment paper

Aluminum foil

DIRECTIONS:

Preheat oven to 350 degrees. Rehydrate soy curls. Drain and remove all water. Add soy curls and all ingredients to a food processor, leaving 1 tablespoon of oil, and process until smooth. On countertop place large piece of aluminum foil, sometimes I double this for two pieces for extra stability, and then place a large piece of parchment over top and coat with the remaining oil. Pour ingredients over parchment paper. Center evenly in a roll and take one side of the parchment paper and place over the loaf mix to make a roll. Then do the aluminum foil in the same manner. Make sure to twist the ends like a piece of taffy would be rolled and place on a cookie sheet and bake for 45-60 minutes. Remove from oven and let sit until cool. Place in refrigerator overnight. Remove paper and aluminum foil, slice and serve.

Pumpkin Cheesecake

-By Melody Prettyman

INGREDIENTS:

1 cup pumpkin

1 cup Florida cane crystals

1 cup coconut milk

2 - 8 oz. containers Tofutti cream cheese

1 tsp pumpkin pie spice

1 Tbsp lemon juice

4 Tbsp arrowroot powder or cornstarch

1 ½ tsp vanilla

DIRECTIONS:

In blender pour all ingredients and blend until creamy smooth. Pour mixture into pan with crust and bake for 40-50 minutes at 350 degrees. Turn oven off and let set in oven for 2 hours. Take out of oven, cover and place in refrigerator overnight.

NOTE: I use a spring pan, but you can make in baking dish and cut into squares.

extra extra

[Cooking Show "Special Gatherings"]

Fun Fruit Mocktails

-By Mark Anthony

INGREDIENTS:

1 part pineapple juice

2 parts raspberry juice

2 parts freshly squeezed orange juice

Lemonade

DIRECTIONS:

Shake all of the juices in a shaker with ice. Strain into a cocktail glass and top up with the lemonade.

Holiday Salad

-By Melody Prettyman

INGREDIENTS:

SALAD

1 lb. red and green lettuce, trimmed and cut into 1-inch circles

1 medium green apple, peeled, cored, and cut into 1-inch cubes

1 avocado, diced into 1-inch cubes

1 Tbsp dried cranberries

2/3 cup defrosted corn kernels

RASPBERRY LEMON DRESSING

1 small package fresh raspberries

½ cup olive oil

¼ cup concentrated white grape raspberry juice

¼ cup Florida cane crystals

½ cup fresh lemon juice

3 Tbsp Black cherry fruit spread, jam

1 Tbsp Dijon mustard, or mustard powder

1 tsp onion powder

1 tsp poppy seed, optional

DIRECTIONS:

Prepare salad in a bowl, cover and refrigerate

SALAD DRESSING

In blender add all ingredients except poppy seeds. Blend until smooth. Add poppy seeds and stir. Pour into a serving container and refrigerate until ready to serve.

extra extra

Artichoke and Spinach Dip

-By Melody Prettyman

INGREDIENTS:

1 - 8 oz. container Tofutti Cream Cheese

1 - 14 oz. can artichoke hearts, drained and coarsely chopped

1/2 cup chopped frozen spinach, thawed

1/4 cup veganaise or favorite vegan mayonnaise

1/4 cup vegan parmesan cheese

1 garlic clove, finely minced

1/2 tsp dried basil

1/4 tsp garlic powder

Salt - to taste

DIRECTIONS:

Allow Tofutti cream cheese to come to room temperature. Cream together veganaise, parmesan style cheese, garlic, basil, and garlic powder. Mix well. Add the artichoke hearts and spinach (be careful to drain this well), and mix until blended. Store in a container until you are ready to use. Spray pie pan with Pam, pour in dip, and top with additional parmesan style cheese and bake at 350 degrees for 25 minutes or until the top is browned. Serve with toasted bread.

Steak Bake

-By Mark Anthony

This is a great meat substitute recipe for soups, beef stew, beef tips, or even a beef roast that can be sliced up for fajitas, or BBQ sandwiches.

INGREDIENTS:

1 cup rice flour

4 1/2 cups vital wheat gluten flour

2 cups mirepoix blended (celery, carrots, onions)

3 cups vegetable stock

1 Tbsp caramel coloring

DIRECTIONS:

Set aside 1/2 cup of vital wheat gluten flour for later use. Stir together the 4 cups vital flour and rice flour. Add the extra fine blended mirepoix, vegetable stock and caramel color and mix well. Mixture should hold together, if not, add a little more vital flour. Place dough in a lightly oiled baking pan, forming into a log shape. Poke some holes into the meat and take the remaining 1 cup of vital flour and sprinkle extra thick over the top, this will simulate fat in the finished product. Close up the holes gently reform it into a log. Add about 1/2 cup of water into the bottom of the pan, cover with foil and bake at 350 degrees for 40 minutes. remove cover and cook for an additional 10 minutes. Cool and cut into desired pieces.

extra extra

Carob-Pumpkin Torte

-By Melody Prettyman

INGREDIENTS:

1 3/4 cup white wheat flour, or all purpose gluten-free flour blend

3/4 cup Florida cane crystals

1/2 cup carob powder

1 Tbsp baking powder, aluminum free

1 tsp pumpkin pie spice

1/2 tsp salt

1 1/3 cup soy, almond or coconut milk

1 Tbsp lemon juice

1 - 15-oz. can unsweetened pumpkin puree

3/4 cup brown sugar, packed, organic

2 Tbsp ground flax seed

1 Tbsp arrowroot powder

1/4 cup olive oil

1/4 cup agave nectar

1 Tbsp vanilla

1 container soya-too whipped topping, whipped and chilled

DIRECTIONS:

Preheat oven to 350. In a medium bowl sift together flour, cane crystals, carob powder, baking powder and pumpkin spice, stir with a wire whisk. Add the salt, arrowroot powder and ground flaxseed, stir ingredients together until blended.

In a separate bowl add milk and lemon juice, stir. Add the pumpkin, brown sugar, oil, agave nectar and vanilla to the milk and blend with a whisk. Add the liquid ingredients to the dry ingredients and stir together until smooth. Pour batter evenly into 2 round cake pans. Bake for 35-40 minutes or insert toothpick, if it comes out clean cakes are ready. Remove from oven and cool for 10 minutes and place on a wire rack until completely cooled. Divide whipped topping and smooth over cake, placing one on top of the other. Use remaining topping to cover top cake. Drizzle with vegan caramel for a beautiful gourmet holiday cake.

[Show "Baking and Beyond"]

Cranberry Orange Scones

INGREDIENTS:

2 cups flour

3 Tbsp natural sugar

1 whole orange zest peel

2 tsp baking powder

1/4 tsp baking soda

1/3 cup cold vegan margarine

1 cup dried cranberries

1/4 cup orange juice

1/4 cup soy milk

1 1/2 tsp prepared egg replacer

DIRECTIONS:

In a bowl, combine the flour, sugar, orange peel, baking powder, and baking soda. Mix well and cut in the margarine until consistent. In another bowl mix the cranberries, orange juice, soy milk, and egg replacer. Mix in the flour mixture and mix until stiff dough forms. On a floured surface, gently knead about 6 times. Pat dough into 10 inch circle, cut into 8 to 10 wedges. Bake at 400 degrees for 12-15 minutes. Great served with a dollop of lemon pie filling.

extra extra

Banana Bread

INGREDIENTS:

3 cups wheat flour

3 tsp baking powder

1/2 tsp baking soda

1 tsp cinnamon

3 tsp prepared egg replacer

6 bananas large mashed

1 1/2 cups honey

1/2 cup applesauce unsweetened

1 cup chopped walnuts or pecans

DIRECTIONS:

Mix dry ingredients and set aside. Mix egg replacer with bananas, honey, apple sauce. Mix in the dry ingredients and add nuts at the end. Makes 6 mini loaves or 2 large loaves. Bake at 350 degrees for 50-60 minutes. Do not overcook, it is actually better to under cook a little bit.

Baked Asparagus & Red Pepper Fritatta

INGREDIENTS:

1 lb. asparagus, tough ends trimmed

Safflower oil, for oiling pan

1 lb. firm tofu, crumbled

1/2 cup soy milk, rice milk, or other non-dairy milk of choice

2 Tbsp arrowroot or cornstarch

2 Tbsp nutritional yeast flakes

1 Tbsp garlic, minced

1 1/2 tsp agar-agar flakes

1 tsp Dijon mustard

1 tsp sea salt

1/4 tsp turmeric

1/8 tsp white pepper

1/4 cup freshly chopped basil

1/4 cup freshly chopped parsley

1/4 cup red pepper, fine diced

1/2 cup green onions, thinly sliced

1/2 cup vegan soy mozzarella cheese, shredded

DIRECTIONS:

Begin by preparing the asparagus: fill a medium saucepan half full with water, place it over high heat, and bring to a boil. Slice the asparagus spears diagonally into 1-inch pieces and place them in a fine mesh strainer. Place the strainer in the boiling water and cook the asparagus in the water for 2 minutes to blanch them. Remove the strainer from the water and set the asparagus aside. Lightly oil a 10-inch quiche pan or springform pan and set aside. In a food processor, place the tofu, soy milk, arrowroot, nutritional yeast flakes, garlic, agar-agar, Dijon mustard, salt, turmeric, and white pepper, and process for 2 minutes or until it forms a smooth puree. Pour half of the tofu mixture into the prepared quiche pan, evenly distribute the blanched asparagus and the remaining ingredients in the pan, and then top with the remaining tofu mixture. Using a spoon, slightly swirl the two mixtures together, and then smooth the top.

Bake at 375 degrees for 35-45 minutes or until the filling is firm to the touch and dry on the top. Remove the frittata from the oven and allow to cool for 10 minutes before cutting. Serve warm, cold, or at room temperature. Garnish with sliced avocado.

Tofu Cream Cheese Frosting

INGREDIENTS:

8 oz. tofu cream cheese, softened

1/3 cup vegan margarine

3 cups powdered sugar

2 tsp vanilla

1 tsp almond extract

DIRECTIONS:

Using an electric mixer or in a large bowl with a hand held mixer, place the tofu cream cheese, and cream them together. Add the sugar, vanilla, and almond extract, and continue to beat the mixture until light and fluffy.

Yield: 2 1/2 cups or enough for two 9" inch layers or a 9"x13" inch cake

Baked Apple Leather

INGREDIENTS:

5 pounds assorted apples

Natural Sugar

Lemon juice

Cinnamon & nutmeg

DIRECTIONS:

Preheat the oven to a low 150 degrees (if your oven doesn't go below 200 degrees, keep oven door propped open slightly). A convection setting will speed up the process and help dry out the puree. Peel, core, and chop the apples. Boil off apples until fully soft. About 10 minutes of boiling time. Drain off water and puree apples until extremely smooth. For every 4 cups of fruit, add about 2 tbsp of sugar and 1 tsp of lemon juice. You may need to add a little water to get an extremely smooth puree. Add cinnamon and nutmeg to taste and extra sugar if needed. Pour apple puree onto a sheet pan lined with plastic wrap. Spread evenly and bake for 8 to 12 hours. The thinner the puree, the quicker it will dry. Let dry in the oven like this for as long as it takes for the puree to dry out and form fruit leather. The baked fruit leather is ready when it is no longer sticky and has a smooth surface.

NOTE: you can add food colorings to get different looks.

[Cooking Show "Pizza Party"]

Vegan Ribs

INGREDIENTS:

3/4 cup vital wheat gluten flour

1/4 cup rice flour

1 cup water

1 tsp garlic powder

1 tsp onion powder

1 Tbsp beef-less base

1 cup BBQ sauce

6 cinnamon sticks

DIRECTIONS:

Mix flours with garlic and onion. In a separate container, mix water with beef-less base. Combine the two into a loose dough that doesn't hold together. If it is holding together too tight, add some water. Spray a sheet pan. We are making the ribs by spreading out the bottom first, about 1/4" thick and 2" by 3". Then place the cinnamon sticks on top. The next step is to put a duplicated layer of the gluten mixture on the top of the cinnamon stick and do a little pressing and forming to create a rib looking product.

Bake In a preheated 300 degree oven for 40 minutes, flipping the ribs every 10 minutes. Now they are ready to fridge, freeze or finish cooking. To finish cooking, splash with BBQ sauce and bake at 400 degrees for about 7 minutes on each side, or grill on the char-broiler, or pan fry to get some glazing on the ribs. This high cooking will give them the real rib look. You can also do another splashing of BBQ sauce right before serving.

Whole Wheat Pizza Dough

INGREDIENTS:

1/4 oz. envelope of dry activated yeast

1/4 cup warm water

1 Tbsp honey

3 3/4 cups whole wheat flour

1 cup water

2 Tbsp olive oil

Pinch of salt

DIRECTIONS:

Dissolve the yeast with the warm water and stir in the honey, let set for 5 minutes. In another bowl, mix cup of water, olive oil and salt. Add the flour and add the yeast mixture. Knead for about 3 minutes and then divide into 2 balls.

Whole Wheat Cauliflower Pizza Dough

INGREDIENTS:

1/4 oz. envelope of dry activated yeast

1/4 cup warm water

1 Tbsp honey

3 3/4 cups whole wheat flour

1 cup water

2 Tbsp olive oil

Pinch of salt

2 cups grated cauliflower (Steamed & Cooled)

DIRECTIONS:

Dissolve the yeast with the warm water and stir in the honey, let set for 5 minutes. In another bowl, mix cup of water, olive oil and salt. Add the flour and add the yeast mixture. Knead for about 3 minutes, mix in the 2 cups of grated cauliflower and then divide into 2 balls.

Pizza Sauce White

INGREDIENTS:

1 - 12oz. pack silken soft tofu

1/2 cup soy milk

1 tsp onion powder

1 tsp minced garlic

½ tsp sea salt

½ tsp natural sugar

1/8 tsp red pepper

1/8 tsp nutmeg

DIRECTIONS:

Blend well in a blender for about three minutes and it's ready to use.

Pizza Sauce Garlic

INGREDIENTS:

1 cup olive oil

¼ cup garlic

½ tsp sea salt

DIRECTIONS:

Mix well for a couple minutes, let set for an hour or a day.

Pizza Sauce Red

INGREDIENTS:

1 - 29 oz. can tomato sauce

1 - 29 oz. can crushed tomatoes

1 - 8 oz. can tomato paste

1/2 tsp salt

1/2 tsp crushed red pepper

1/4 cup sugar

1/4 cup basil

1/8 cup oregano

1 Tbsp fennel

DIRECTIONS:

Mix all the ingredients together and simmer for 1 hour. Use right away or chill overnight to use for pastas.

[Cooking Show "Flavor"]

Italian Vegan Cutlets

INGREDIENTS:

½ gallon water

½ cup Bragg's Liquid Aminos

¼ cup garlic

2 cups vital wheat gluten flour

2 cups cool water

2 cups bread crumbs

¼ cup Italian seasoning

Olive oil for sauté

DIRECTIONS:

Bring to boil the 1/2 gallon water with Bragg's and garlic. In a bowl mix the vital wheat gluten with 2 cups cool water until it forms a ball. Roll out into a log form, on a cutting board and let rest for ten minutes. Then cut ½ inch slices and put into the boiling water. Keep covered with lid stirring occasionally. Be careful not to boil over. Drain water and try to squeeze out a bit. Mix the bread crumbs and Italian seasoning. Bread the cutlets and sauté.

extra extra

Italian Infused Olive Oil

INGREDIENTS:

1 cup olive oil

2 Tbsp basil

2 Tbsp oregano

1 Tbsp tarragon

1 Tbsp garlic powder

1 Tbsp onion powder

1 tsp sea salt

DIRECTIONS:

In a sauce pan, take ½ cup olive oil and all the ingredients and mix together. Cook over low heat just until the mixture starts to bubble. Pull aside and let set for about 15 minutes for the oil to absorb the flavors. Add the additional oil and strain the oil through a cheese cloth or filter. Use oil for dipping, cooking or salads.

Marinated Asparagus Salad

INGREDIENTS:

10 oz. pkg. frozen asparagus (or fresh)

1/2 cup olive oil

1/3 cup lemon juice

1 pack Italian dressing mix

3 Tbsp green pepper, fine diced

3 Tbsp chopped radish, fine chopped

1 Tbsp parsley chopped

1 Tbsp chopped chives

1 head Boston lettuce

4 thick tomato slices

4 red pepper strips

DIRECTIONS:

Blanch off asparagus in boiling water for 2 minutes and then shock with cold water to keep the color green and stop the cooking process. In a container with a lid, mix oil, lemon juice, salad dressing and shake well. Add green peppers, radishes, parsley, chives, and asparagus; toss a couple times and refrigerate overnight. Drain and keep reserve marinade. Line 4 salad plates with lettuce, place tomato slice on lettuce, and top with asparagus spears. Gather together into a bundle and arrange red pepper strips to look like ties. Pour remaining dressing over salad.

Francese Sauce

INGREDIENTS:

2 cups water

1 Tbsp chicken-less base

4 Tbsp lemon juice

2 Tbsp vegan margarine

2 Tbsp lemon zest

3 Tbsp honey

2 Tbsp natural sugar crystals

¼ cup fresh chopped parsley

¼ cup fresh chopped green onions

1/8 cup plain soy milk

Cornstarch and water slurry

DIRECTIONS:

Bring to a boil the water, chicken-less base, lemon juice, vegan butter, lemon zest, honey, and Florida crystals. Thicken with slurry. Add the parsley and green onions and let set for 5 minutes to absorb the flavors. Add soy milk to give it a creamy effect.

Marsala Sauce

(alcohol free)

INGREDIENTS:

2 cups mushrooms (sliced)

¼ cup shallots

1 tsp garlic crushed

2 Tbsp olive oil

½ tsp vegan beef base

1 cup grape juice

¼ tsp sea salt

Pinch sage

Pinch thyme

Cornstarch & water slurry

DIRECTIONS:

Sauté the mushrooms, shallots and garlic with the olive oil. Add the remaining ingredients and bring to a boil. Simmer for about 15 minutes.
Thicken with cornstarch slurry.

extra extra

Banana Foster

INGREDIENTS:

4 Tbsp vegan margarine

2 cups brown sugar

¼ tsp nutmeg

1/8 tsp allspice

¼ tsp vanilla

¼ tsp lemon juice

4 bananas

DIRECTIONS:

Take all ingredients except the bananas and simmer over medium heat until smooth and incorporated. Add long sliced bananas and cook for only one minute. Pour over ice cream or short cake.

[Cooking Show "Fun Foods"]

Pinwheel Sandwiches

INGREDIENTS:

8 Tbsp vegan cream cheese

4 10-inch wheat flour tortillas

1/4 cup alfalfa sprouts

1/2 cup shredded romaine

1/2 cup sliced avocado

1/2 cup fire roasted red bell pepper

1/4 cup chopped tomatoes

1/2 cup diced cucumbers

1/2 cup red onion (fine slivers)

Salt and pepper, to taste

DIRECTIONS:

Spread one tablespoon of cream cheese over each tortilla. Sprinkle an even amount of the remaining ingredients on each wrap; roll up. And now the fun part, splash with BBQ sauce for a BBQ wrap, Asian sauces for Asian wrap, pesto sauces for an Italian wrap, salsa for a Mexican wrap.

Makes 4 servings.

extra extra

Cucumber Salad Cylinders

INGREDIENTS:

2 cucumbers (long English cucumbers)

1 cup cucumber (peeled and diced)

1 avocado (small slivers)

¼ cup onion (small slivers)

4 strawberries (thin sliced)

1 green apple diced

¼ cup dried cranberries

1 Tbsp lemon juice

BASIL INFUSED OLIVE OIL

¼ cup olive oil

1 tsp crushed garlic

¼ tsp sea salt

2 Tbsp fresh basil

1 Tbsp cilantro

1/8 tsp red pepper flakes

DIRECTIONS:

Take the cucumbers and slice a couple good slices out of the middle. I use a slicer, but you can use a knife or using a wide vegetable peeler will give you a consistent slice. We will save the rest of the cucumber for the filling. We are going to curve the cucumber and then you can attach them together with a decorative pick. What I do is just do an angle cut on each end and then hook them together. Then take the diced apples and splash with the lemon juice and mix in well. This will keep them from turning brown. For the diced cucumbers, I use the leftovers from the slices that I took out of the cucumbers. For the strawberries, slice off the stems and then do a thin flat slice so you can get the strawberry shape. Gently mix in all the additional ingredients and gently place in the cucumber cylinder. You can also add nuts for a crunchy addition. Splash with the infused olive oil.

Stuffed Pumpkins

INGREDIENTS:

2 small pumpkins or baby pumpkins

4 Tbsp vegan butter blend

3 onions, minced

3 celery stalks, diced

3 carrots, diced

1 tsp salt

½ cup water

3 cups brown rice, cooked

1 tsp rosemary

½ tsp rubbed sage

½ cup roasted pumpkin seeds

DIRECTIONS:

Cut off the tops and scoop out the seeds and membranes. Set aside. Preheat the oven to 350°F. Heat 1 Tbsp of the oil in a large skillet. Sauté the onions until lightly browned. Add the celery and carrots and sauté for a few minutes. Add the salt and water. Simmer for 10 minutes. Add the rice, rosemary, sage, and roasted pumpkin seeds. Fill the pumpkin shells with the rice mixture. Place in a baking dish and cover with foil. Bake for 1 1/2 hours, or until the pumpkin sides are soft enough to eat but are not collapsing.

extra extra

Chocolate Avocado Pudding

INGREDIENTS:

6 avocados

2 cups maple syrup

2 cups carob powder

2 tsp vanilla

DIRECTIONS:

Using a mixing bowl, slowly mix the maple syrup, vanilla, and carob powder. Add the avocados and begin to mix faster and faster until you are able to whip on high. Whip on high for about 2 minutes. I like to chill for a couple hours and then whip it again on high for a couple more minutes. This helps make it fluffier and more incorporated.

Popcorn Balls

INGREDIENTS:

2 cups sugar

1 1/3 cups water

1/2 cup light corn syrup

1 tsp lemon juice

1/2 tsp salt

1 tsp vanilla extract

18 cups popped corn

DIRECTIONS:

In a sauce pot, bring sugar, water, lemon juice and corn syrup to a boil. With a candy thermometer, heat to 255 degrees. Add salt and vanilla. We are going to lightly drizzle the mixture over the popcorn, mixing often. Lightly oil your hands or spray with pan spray. As the mixture cools to a temperature that is safe and able to handle, you will be able to form into popcorn balls. Form into any sizes you want. I like to wrap them with a clear wrap and ribbon.

[MARK & MELODY COOKING PROGRAM: *"Going Nuts"*]

Almondaise

-by Melody Prettyman

INGREDIENTS:

1 cup water

½ cup almonds, blanched

½ cup water

½ tsp salt

1 tsp onion powder

1 tsp mustard powder

½ cup olive oil

2 Tbsp lemon juice

DIRECTIONS:

In small sauce pan bring 1 cup of water and the ½ cup of almonds to a boil. Remove from heat. Rinse almonds with cold water and remove skins.

In a blender add; blanched almonds, ½ cup water, salt, onion powder and mustard powder. Blend on high speed until creamy. Slowly drizzle in olive oil while blender is still on high speed. Blend for 1-2 additional minutes. Pour mixture into small bowl. Add lemon juice stirring with whisk until creamy. Refrigerate in storage container or pint jar.

Almondaise Tartar Sauce

-by Melody Prettyman

INGREDIENTS:

1/3 cup almondaise

2 Tbsp heaping red onions, diced fine

1 Tbsp dill relish

DIRECTIONS:

In a small bowl add almondaise, diced onions and dill relish. Mix and serve or store in an airtight container in refrigerator.

Almond Milk

-by Melody Prettyman

INGREDIENTS:

1 cup blanched almonds, see note

½ tsp salt

2 Tbsp agave nectar

Quart water

DIRECTIONS:

In a small pan bring 1 cup water and almonds to a boil. Remove from heat and rinse with cold water. Remove skin. In a blender mix all ingredients until creamy. Pour mixture into a nut bag or cheese cloth and strain milk from pulp. Store milk in an airtight container in refrigerator.

NOTE: Keep nut pulp to make almond cookies.

Cashew Nut Crusted Tofu

-by Melody Prettyman

INGREDIENTS:

2 - 14 oz. containers water packed tofu, sliced (see note)

2 Tbsp olive oil

½ cup cashews, raw

1/3 cup yeast flakes

1 tsp McKay's chicken style seasoning, vegan special

1 Tbsp parsley flakes

½ tsp salt

2 Tbsp Earth Balance margarine

2 ½ cups bread crumbs, (see note)

DIRECTIONS:

Preheat oven to 350 degrees. Line a cookie sheet with aluminum foil. Spray the foil with non stick spray. Place the slices of tofu on the foiled pan and bake in oven for 15- 20 minutes. Remove and leave sit.

In a food processor add; cashews, yeast flakes, chicken style seasoning, and salt, process for 2-3 minutes. Add to bread crumbs and parsley and mix well. Brush both sides of tofu with olive oil, place one spoonful of nut crumb mixture over one side of the tofu, place face down on the covered cookie sheet and place another spoonful of nut crumb mix over the top. Pat mixture down onto the tofu and continue until all mixture is on both bottom and top of all the tofu. Place back in oven and bake for an additional 15-20 minutes, until golden brown. Let cool for a few minutes and place onto plate. Add a spoonful of Almondaise tartar sauce to the top and serve.

NOTE: Bread crumbs: I place 3-4 slices of bread in the food processor and blend until fine. Place on a cookie sheet for 1-2 hours to dry.

TOFU: I slice tofu in 3 slices to make a 3x4 inch slice.

Pecan Tofu Loaf

-by Melody Prettyman

INGREDIENTS:

1 lb. raw pecans, chopped

2 large onions, diced

2 - 14-oz. pkgs. organic tofu

1 - 12-oz. container tofutti sour cream

3 Tbsp soy or earth balance margarine

3 Tbsp Mckays chicken style seasoning, vegan special

1 Tbsp vege-sal

1 Tbsp onion powder

1 box organic corn cereal, juice sweetened preferred, (I use Natures Path)

1 cup vegetable broth

2 Tbsp arrowroot powder

DIRECTIONS:

Preheat oven to 350 degrees.
Step 1- Rinse and squeeze water from the tofu. In a bowl, crumble tofu. Add the tofutti sour cream and mix well. Set aside. Step 2- in a 9"x13" prepared casserole dish add the tofu mixture, diced pecans, arrow- root powder and cereal. Steps 3- In a skillet add Earth Balance, onions, Mckays chicken style seasoning, vege-sal and onion powder. Sauté on medium heat until onions are transparent. Add 4 cups of vegetable broth to the onion mixture, stir and pour over the nut mixture. Mix all ingredients well. Bake covered for 45 minutes. Remove lid, or foil and bake an additional 10-15 minutes until golden brown. Serve warm.

Almond & Dried Cherry Iced Cookies

-by Melody Prettyman

INGREDIENTS:

½ cup Earth Balance or soy margarine, room temperature

½ cup plus 1 Tbsp organic cane sugar

½ cup almond pulp (see note)

1/4 cup fresh almond milk

1 tsp almond flavoring

1 tsp vanilla

½ tsp salt

½ cup dried cherries, diced

½ cup almond slices, roasted

1 ½ cups unbleached or white wheat flour, sifted

ICING:

½ cup organic confectioner sugar

1 ½ Tbsp almond milk

1 tsp Earth Balance margarine

1/8 tsp almond flavoring (just a drop)

DIRECTIONS:

Preheat oven to 350°
In medium size mixing bowl add; margarine, sugar, almond pulp, and almond milk. Using a whisk, mix until smooth. Add almond flavoring, vanilla, salt and cherries, mix well. Add almonds and sifted flour and mix. Spoon cookie dough onto a cookie sheet and bake for 12-15 minutes. Remove from oven let set for a few minutes, drizzle over cookies while cookies are still warm. Place on platter and serve. Makes approximately 24 cookies

NOTE: When making almond milk I save the pulp squeezed from the nut bag and use it to make these cookies

[Cooking Show - American BBQ]

Vinegar Free BBQ Sauce

INGREDIENTS:

2 cups ketchup

¼ cup mustard

¼ cup brown sugar

¼ cup water

2 Tbsp honey

1 tsp vinegar free pepper sauce

1 tsp Bragg's liquid aminos

1 tsp paprika

1 tsp garlic powder

1 tsp onion powder

½ tsp salt

½ tsp liquid smoke

DIRECTIONS:

Mix ingredients and simmer on low for 15 minutes.

extra extra

Black Bean Oatmeal Burgers

INGREDIENTS:

2 1/2 cups water

1 1/4 cups onions, minced

1 tsp garlic, minced

1/4 cup olive oil

2 Tbsp beef-less base

6 Tbsp Bragg's liquid aminos

3 cups old fashioned oatmeal

1 - 14-oz. can black beans drained and mashed

1 - 14-oz. can beets minced with juice

DIRECTIONS:

Boil water, onions, garlic, olive oil, beef-less base and Bragg's Liquid Aminos for 15 minutes. Add oatmeal and let rest off the heat for 10 minutes. Mix in beans and beets with juice and let rest 5 minutes. Mix a little and form into burger patties.
Grill or charbroil.

Southern Potato Salad

-by Melody Prettyman

INGREDIENTS:

6-8 potatoes, boiled and diced

3 stalks of celery, diced

1 onion, diced

3 carrots, diced

1/4 cup sweet pickles, diced

1 cup prepared vegan mayonnaise or veganaise

1 Tbsp ground mustard

1 tsp salt

1 Tbsp Florida cane crystals

Sprinkle of paprika

DIRECTIONS:

Dice boiled potatoes into a large bowl. Add remaining ingredients and mix well. Sprinkle a little paprika over the top of potato salad when it is done for added color. Chill in refrigerator before serving.

All American Apple Pie Ala Mode

-by Melody Prettyman

PIE INGREDIENTS:

1 oatmeal pie crust for a 9 inch double crust pie or gluten free pie crust

1/4 cup Earth Balance margarine

3 Tbsp arrowroot powder or cornstarch

1/3 cup concentrated apple juice

1/2 cup packed organic brown sugar

1 tsp fresh lemon juice

1 tsp vanilla

Dash nutmeg

1 tsp cinnamon

8 Granny Smith apples - peeled, cored and sliced

DIRECTIONS:

Preheat oven to 350 degrees. In sauce pan add; Earth Balance margarine, arrowroot powder, apple juice, brown sugar, vanilla, nutmeg and cinnamon and bring to a boil. Reduce temperature and let simmer. Place the bottom crust in your pan. Fill with apples, mounded slightly. Cover with a lattice work of crust. Gently pour the sugar and butter liquid over the crust. Pour slowly so that it does not run off.

Bake for 40-60 minutes, until apples are soft.

Soy Ice Cream

by Melody Prettyman

INGREDIENTS:

1 cup soy milk

1 box firm silken tofu

½ cup cashews raw, rinsed

½ - ¾ cup Florida cane crystals

½ cup coconut milk

3 Tbsp Better Than Milk powder, original

1 tsp vanilla powder

½ tsp salt

DIRECTIONS:

In blender add all ingredients. Start blender out on low and then turn to high speed. If you do not have a high powered blender like a Vita-mix you want to make sure the nuts are creamy. Blend for 4-5 minutes. Place in a freezer storage container until frozen or ready to use. I will remove from freezer and let sit for just a few minutes before serving.

CAROB ICE-CREAM:
Add 2 tablespoons of carob powder to half the batter, blend for an additional 1-2 minutes.

STRAWBERRY ICE-CREAM:
Blend an additional ½ cup of cashews at the beginning of the process to add additional fat because of the fruit. Add 1½ cup frozen strawberries and blend for 2-3 minutes or until strawberries are smooth. Dice ½ cup frozen or fresh strawberries and add to the mix and stir with spoon. Freeze and serve.

Sauces for Ice Cream and Banana Splits

-by Melody Prettyman

Carob Sauce

INGREDIENTS:

1 cup coconut milk, canned

1 cup carob chips, vegan malted sweetened

1/3 cup Florida cane crystals

¼ soy milk

2 Tbsp arrowroot powder

DIRECTIONS:

In blender combine all ingredients until creamy smooth. In a medium sauce pan bring to a simmer for 2-3 minutes stirring continuously. Pour into a small serving bowl to cool. Serve over your favorite ice-cream.

Strawberry Sauce

-by Melody Prettyman

INGREDIENTS:

1 cup trozen concentrated white grape juice, fruit sweetened

3 cups frozen or fresh strawberries

2 Tbsp arrowroot powder

¼ cup Florida cane crystals

1/8 cup water

DIRECTIONS:

In a medium sauce pan bring grape juice, strawberries and cane crystals to a boil. Simmer for 4-5 minutes. Make slurry with the arrowroot powder and water, stir and add to berry mixture stirring continuously.

extra extra

Banana Split

-by Melody Prettyman

INGREDIENTS:

1 scoop strawberry soy ice-cream

1 scoop carob soy ice-cream

1 banana sliced in half, length

2-3 Tbsp carob sauce

2-3 Tbsp strawberry sauce

¼ cup soy whipped topping

2-3 Tbsp toasted pecans, diced fine

2- cherries, fresh

1 banana split boat-dish

DIRECTIONS:

Slice banana in half length wise and place in dish. Take 1 scoop of carob soy ice-cream and 1 scoop of strawberry soy ice-cream. Cover carob ice-cream with carob sauce, cover strawberry ice-cream with strawberry sauce. Cover with soy whipped topping and sprinkle with toasted pecans and cherries on top.

ENJOY!

[Cooking Program - Asian Grille]

Teriyaki Glaze

INGREDIENTS:

1 1/2 cups pineapple juice

1 cup orange juice

1 tsp ginger minced

¼ cup Bragg's liquid aminos

1/4 cup soy sauce

1 Tbsp sugar

DIRECTIONS:

Slurry mix of 4 tbsp corn starch & 4 tbsp water.

Mix ingredients together and bring to a boil for 5 minutes. Whisk in slurry to thicken.

Sweet and Sour Sauce

INGREDIENTS:

1 - 29 oz. can fruit cocktail

1 - 20 oz. can pineapple chunks

1 - 24 oz. jar maraschino cherries

DIRECTIONS:

Slurry mix of 1/4 cup cornstarch & 1/4 cup Water

Mix ingredients together and bring to a boil for 5 minutes. Whisk in slurry to thicken.

extra extra

Orange Glaze

INGREDIENTS:

1 1/2 cups water

1 1/2 cups orange juice

1/4 cup lemon juice

2 Tbsp Bragg's liquid aminos

2 Tbsp orange zest

1 Tbsp ginger, fresh minced

1/4 tsp salt

DIRECTIONS:

Slurry mix of 3 tbsp cornstarch & 3 tbsp water.

Mix ingredients together and bring to a boil for 5 minutes. Whisk in slurry to thicken.

Lemon Sauce

INGREDIENTS:

1 cup water

1/4 cup lemon juice

2 Tbsp lemon zest

4 Tbsp sugar

4 Tbsp honey

DIRECTIONS:

Slurry mix of 2 tbsp cornstarch & 2 tbsp water.

Mix ingredients together and bring to a boil for 5 minutes. Whisk in slurry to thicken.

Red Pepper Pesto

INGREDIENTS:

1 cup fire roasted red bell peppers

1 Tbsp minced garlic

Pinch salt

DIRECTIONS:

Blend into a paste with a food processor.

Asian Poached Pears

INGREDIENTS:

4 Bartlett pears

1/2 cup orange glaze

1 cup favorite granola mix

1/8 cup coconut flakes

DIRECTIONS:

Take the pears, peel and core. Freeze overnight. Thaw and stuff with granola mixture of dried fruit, nuts and granola. Top with orange glaze and coconut.

[Veggie Fountain Cooking Program]

Hot Grain Delight

INGREDIENTS:

1 cup hard red wheat

1 cup brown rice

5 cups water

DIRECTIONS:

Crock-pot on low overnight and it's ready.

Add a pinch of salt if you like.

Top with your favorite toppings; honey, soy milk, fruit, nuts, etc.

Breakfast Sausages

INGREDIENTS:

1 cup white kidney beans, rinsed and drained

1 cup veggie broth

2 Tbsp olive oil

2 Tbsp Bragg's liquid aminos

2 Tbsp maple syrup

1/4 cup nutritional yeast flakes

1 tsp paprika

1 Tbsp sage

Pinch cayenne

1/2 tsp thyme

1/2 tsp rosemary

1/2 tsp whole fennel seed

1/2 cup soaked TVP

1 1/4 cups vital wheat gluten flour

DIRECTIONS:

Mash beans and add the top ingredients. Mix well.
Add the TVP and wheat gluten. Mix very well and set aside.
Take about a ping pong ball size amount and wrap with foil just like a tootsie roll.
Place in oven water bath for 25 minutes at 350 degrees.
Allow to cool a little and unwrap.
Optional reheat on the grill. Great for creating the grill markings.

Millet Creations

INGREDIENTS:

2 cans frozen concentrate juice

8 cups water

1 Tbsp salt (optional)

2 cups millet flour

1 can berry pie filling

2 cups granola

1/2 cup coconut flakes

DIRECTIONS:

½ of the juice mixture is brought to a boil. And the other ½ is mixed with the millet flour and salt.
Add the flour mixture to the boiling juice and stir until boil returns.
Simmer for 20 minutes on low.
Place in glass baking dish or individual serving bowls.
Chill for 4 hours.
Top with a berry pie filling, granola and coconut flakes.

Spinach Enchiladas

INGREDIENTS:

1/2 cup olive oil

1/2 cup onions

1 tsp sea salt

2 tsp seasoning salt

2 - 10 oz. package frozen chopped spinach

2 - 10 oz. package whole leaf spinach

2 cups vegan mozzarella cheese, shredded

1/2 cup pecans or other nuts

2 - 14oz. can enchilada sauce, mild

12 corn tortillas

DIRECTIONS:

Sauté onions in the garlic and olive oil.

Add the salts, spinach and nuts. Mix and set aside.

Dip the tortillas in hot oil and set aside.

Take the spinach mixture and add ½ of the cheese and evenly roll the mixture into the tortillas.

Place in a glass baking pan.

Top the enchiladas with sauce and remaining cheese.

Bake for 30 minutes at 350 degrees.

extra extra

Chicken Fried Steaks

FOR THE MEAT:

1 1/2 cup gluten flour

1/2 cup rice flour

2 cups water

6 Tbsp Bragg's liquid aminos

2 Tbsp granulated garlic

2 Tbsp powdered onion

2 Tbsp beef-less base

YOU WILL ALSO NEED:

2 cup bread crumbs

1 tsp sea salt

2 cups flour

1 package tofu (any style works)

1 cup soy milk

FOR THE STEAKS:

Mix the wet ingredients and add the dry, making a mock steak.
Bake steaks in oven at 350 degrees for 5 minutes on each side.
The breading process is first into the flour, second into the tofu milk wash, and third into the bread crumbs.
For the soy milk wash, blend together the tofu and soy milk.
For the bread crumbs, add salt and mix.
Make sure to press the bread crumbs.
Pan-fry in coconut oil on each side for 3 to 5 minutes, or until golden brown.

[Cooking Show - Spring Camp 2009]

Berry & Peach Fruit Topping

INGREDIENTS:

4 cups strawberries, cleaned & diced

2 cups blueberries

4 cups peaches, pealed and diced

1/2 cup brown rice syrup

DIRECTIONS:

Refrigerate and mix occasionally.

Raspberry Tofu Cream Topping

INGREDIENTS:

1 - 12.3 oz. pkg. Mori-Nu silken style tofu, extra firm

1/4 cup raspberry juice concentrate

2 Tbsp sugar or honey

DIRECTIONS:

Blend and refrigerate.

Stuffed French Toast

INGREDIENTS:

BATTER

¾ cup soy milk

1 - 12.3 oz. pkg. silken style soft tofu

1 tsp cinnamon

1 Tbsp vanilla

8 pieces Texas toast

STUFFING

1 cup vegan cream cheese

1/4 cup diced canned peaches

DIRECTIONS:

Split bread and stuff with thin spread of filling. Soak bread in mixture until completely wet. Cook on med-high in oiled pan. Top with berry and peach fruit topping and raspberry tofu topping.

Homemade Spinach Tortillas

INGREDIENTS:

1 cup spinach juice, warm

2 cups flour

2 Tbsp olive oil

1 tsp salt

Pinch of baking soda

DIRECTIONS:

Mix the spinach juice, olive oil and salt, add flour until well mixed into a dough ball. Flatten and pan-fry in a little olive oil.

extra extra

Beef-less Wellington

INGREDIENTS:

3/4 cup vital wheat gluten flour

¼ cup rice flour

1 cup water

3 Tbsp Bragg's liquid aminos

1 Tbsp granulated garlic

1 Tbsp powdered onion

1 Tbsp vegetable base

Sauté Items

1/4 cup mushrooms, sliced

1/4 cup onion, slivers

2 Tbsp olive oil

1 tsp rosemary

1 tsp thyme

1/2 cup vegan brown gravy

1 sheet puff pastry dough

DIRECTIONS:

Mix the wet ingredients and add the dry, making a mock steak.
Cook steaks in oven for 7 minutes on each side.

DIRECTIONS:

Sauté items and set aside.

DIRECTIONS:

To make wellingtons, top steaks with sautéed onions and mushrooms. Add a tablespoon of gravy and wrap with puff pastry dough. Bake for about 40 minutes at 350 degrees. Serve atop the gravy.

Pinto Bean Fudge

INGREDIENTS:

1 cup cooked pinto beans, drained

3/4 cup vegan butter substitute

1 cup carob chips

1 Tbsp vanilla

1 cup chopped walnuts

2 lb. powdered sugar

DIRECTIONS:

Mash beans well, add butter, carob chips and vanilla. Cook until melted and very warm. Gradually add sugar and walnuts. Stir and press into lightly oiled 9"x13" pan, cover and refrigerate.

recipe
index

1000 Island Sauce 185	BBQ Jack Fruit Sandwiches 236
African Sweet Potato Soup. 171	Bean Stuffed Cabbage Rolls 289
Aioli 185	Beef-less Wellington 387
All American Apple Pie Ala Mode 371	Beet Cake with
Almond & Dried Cherry Iced Cookies. 367	Peanut Butter -N- Banana Sauce 312
Almond Ancho Sauce 187	Berry & Peach Fruit Topping. 384
Almond Maple Granola 115	Bird's Nests 332
Almond Milk 364	Black Bean and Lentil Burgers 248
Almondaise 363	Black Bean Hummus. 210
Almondaise Tartar Sauce. 364	Black Bean Oatmeal Burgers. 369
Apple Cider Syrup 195	Black Bean Salsa 203
Apple Fennel Mustard. 189	Black Bean Thai Burger. 242
Applesauce Muffins 91	Black Olive Hummus 211
Artichoke and Spinach Dip 339	Blueberry Sauce 194
Asian Poached Pears. 378	Blueberry Tofu Blend. 137
Asian Tofu Salad. 147	Blueberry-Oat Bars. 316
Avocado Mango Bruschetta 217	Breakfast Sausages. 380
Avocado-Chili Spread. 191	Butternut Soup 169
Baked Apple Leather. 346	Cajun BBQ Sauce 185
Baked Asparagus & Red Pepper Fritatta . . . 344	Cajun Grilled Tofu 230
Balsamic & Sun-dried Bruschetta 220	Cajun Seasoning Rub 230
Balsamic Mustard Sauce. 188	Caribbean Vegetable Stew 172
Banana Bread 343	Carob Chip Cookies. 320
Banana Cookies. 318	Carob Sauce 373
Banana Date Nut Muffins 93	Carob-Pumpkin Torte 341
Banana Foster 357	Cashew Nut Crusted Tofu 365
Banana Ice Cream 301	Chicken Fried Steaks. 383
Banana Pudding Oatmeal. 102	Chicken-less Chicken Salad 240
Banana Split 375	Chili Sauce 192
Banana-Coconut Bars 321	Chinese 5 Spice Ketchup. 188
Banana-Peanut Butter Sauce 313	Chipotle Lime Dressing. 155
Basic Granola Recipe. 112	Chipotle Sauce 192
Basic Stuffed Cabbage Rolls Recipe 287	Chocolate a l'Orange Mousse Pie 315
Basic Tofu Eggs 98	Chocolate Avocado Pudding. 361
Basic Vinaigrette. 193	Chunky Date Granola. 116
Basil Veganaise 193	Cocktail Sauce. 188

recipe index

Corn & Bean Burgers with Chipotle Ketchup 250
Cranberry Orange Scones. 342
Crepes 97
Crock-Pot Almond Joy Oatmeal. 103
Crock-Pot Grain Delight 107
Crock-pot Oil Free Vegan Gumbo. 177
Crock-pot Pumpkin Pie 304
Crock-pot Rice Minestrone 176
Crock-pot Split Pea. 178
Cucumber Salad Cylinders 359
Cucumber Salsa. 191
Curried Tofu Soup 164
Curry Ketchup 188
Delicious Orange Pancakes. 132
Double-Layer Pumpkin Cheesecake 314
Easy Black Bean Sloppy Joe 239
Easy Italian Dressings 153
Easy Mango Salsa 204
Eggless Egg and Garden Veggie Salad. . . . 238
Fast Chocolate Sauce. 194
Fat Free B.O.M. Cookies. 317
Fat-Free Lemon Pie 307
Fat-Free Pumpkin Cookies. 324
Fig Bars. 122
Francese Sauce 355
Fresh Homemade Tomato Juice 140
Fruit Chutney 186
Fun Fruit Mocktails 337
Ginger-Herb Chutney 186
Gingery Split Pea Soup 167
Gluten-Soy Free Cheese Cake. 319
Greek Lima Bean Dip 206
Greek Stuffed Cabbage Rolls. 292
Green Bean Casserole, Vegan Style 331
Green Tomato & Corn Relish. 187
Grilled Chili-Lime Sweet Potatoes. 228
Grilled Lemon-Basil Tofu Burgers 246
Grilled Peach Cobbler 232
Grilled Spinach & Sun-dried Tomato Pizza . 226
Hoisin BBQ Sauce 185
Holiday Salad 338
Homemade Maple Syrup 129
Homemade Spinach Tortillas 386
Hominy-Pinto Burgers with Roasted Poblano Chilies. 251
Honey Banana Dressing 190
Hot Grain Delight. 379
Italian Infused Olive Oil 353
Italian Vegan Cutlets. 352
Italian Verde Sauce. 194
Jalapeno Tartar Sauce 192
Jamaican Jerk Ketchup 189
Kiwi Honeydew Blend 139
Kraut Sauce. 191
Lemon Achiote Grilled Tofu Recipe. 231
Lemon Sauce. 377
Lentil Crusted Faux Scallops 274
Lentil-Barley Burgers with Fiery Fruit Salsa . . 244
Light Bean Salad 145
Low-Fat Sugar Granola. 114
Low-Fat Red Pepper Hummus 212
Low-Fat Blueberry Muffins 89
Low-Fat Creamy "Caesar" Dressing Dip . . . 156
Low-Fat Peanut Butter Banana Cookies . . . 318
Marinated Asparagus Salad 354
Marsala Sauce. 356
Mexican Stew Bread Bowls 163
Middle Eastern Cabbage Rolls. 290
Middle Eastern Potato Chickpea Burgers . . 256
Millet Creations 381
Miso Ginger Sauce. 191
Mock Egg Salad Sandwiches. 237

Mushroom Bruschetta 219
Mustard Dill Sauce 189
No Fat Drop Biscuits. 94
Oatmeal Breakfast Bars 121
Oatmeal Raisin Pancakes 131
Oil-Free Pumpkin Bread 309
Oil-Free Balsamic Vinaigrette 154
Olive Oil Dressing 145
Open-Faced Falafel Burgers 253
Orange Glaze 377
Peach Cobbler Cake. 306
Peach Time Mustard 190
Peanut Sauce 191
Pecan Tofu Loaf 366
Peppercorn-Shallot Sauce 187
Pickle Sauce. 192
Pineapple Salsa 190
Pineapple Salsa 205
Pineapple Sorbet Simplicity 302
Pinto Bean Fudge 388
Pinwheel Sandwiches 358
Pizza Sauce Garlic 350
Pizza Sauce Red 351
Pizza Sauce White 350
Polish Stuffed Cabbage Rolls 291
Popcorn Balls. 362
Portobello Burgers 243
Potato Simplicity. 265
Pumpkin Cheesecake 336
Pumpkin Granola 113
Pumpkin Leather Roll-Ups 311
Pumpkin Soup 165
Quick & Simple Black Bean Burger 252
Quick Cole Slaw Sauce 193
Quick Pico de Gallo 190
Quinoa Hot Breakfast Cereal 108
Raspberry Banana Tofu Muffins 85
Raspberry Cranberry Sauce 330
Raspberry Tofu Cream Topping 384
Red Basil Mocktail 329
Red Onion Relish 186
Red Pepper Pesto 378
Red-Lentil Mushroom Burger with Aioli 254
Relish 187
Rice Simplicity 263
Roasted Corn Guacamole. 204
Roasted Garlic Mustard 189
Roasted Tomato Salsa 190
RootBeer BBQ Sauce 186
Savory Vegetable Stuffed Cabbage 288
Scallion Ketchup. 189
Simple Bruschetta Topping 219
Simple Dijon Salad Dressing 157
Simple Dough Recipe 227
Simple Golden Pancakes. 129
Simple Honey Mustard 190
Simple Hummus 211
Simple Lemon Sauce. 195
Simple No Cook Icing 325
Simple Tofu Spread. 240
Simple Tomato Sauce 185
Simple Vegetable Grilling 225
Simple Whole Wheat Waffles. 130
Slow Cooker Lemon Blueberry Oatmeal . . . 105
Southern Potato Salad. 370
Soy Ice Cream 372
Soy Orange Sauce 188
Spice Grilled Tofu. 229
Spiced Peanut Butter Ketchup 188
Spicy Crock-pot Potato Pea Soup 179
Spicy Duck Sauce. 192
Spicy Orange Cranberry Salsa. 203

recipe index

Spicy Red Pepper Hummus 210
Spinach & Pesto Lasagna 272
Spinach Enchiladas. 382
Spinach Hummus. 211
Spinach Pesto Pasta and Grilled Zucchini . . 277
Steak Bake. 340
Strawberry Sauce 373
Stuffed Cabbage Roll Simplicity 282
Stuffed French Toast 385
Stuffed Pumpkins 360
Stuffed Tomatoes 281
Stuffing 333
Sun-dried Tomato Ketchup 189
Sun-dried Tomato Pizza. 226
Sweet and Sour Sauce 376
Sweet and Spicy Glazed Cashews 326
Sweet Potato Fries. 199
Tangy Steakless Sauce. 186
Ten Minute Tuscan White Bean Soup 166
Teriyaki Glaze 376
Tex-Mex Black Bean Dip/Spread 206
Thai Curry Sauce 191
Thai Papaya Salad 149
The Old Bay Sauce. 187
Tofu Cream Cheese Frosting 345
Tofu Relish 187
Totally Awesome Turkey Loaf 335
Ultimate Cheese Sauce. 196
Ultimate Gourmet Bars 120
Ultimate Meatballs 200
Ultimate Ranch. 158
Vanilla Sauce. 195
Veg-Confetti Muffins 87
Vegan Country Gravy 95
Vegan Crock-pot Stuffing 268
Vegan Eggnog Cheesecake. 310

Vegan Pumpkin Pie. 305
Vegan Ribs. 347
Vegetable Burgers 247
Vegetable Simplicity 261
Vinegar Free BBQ Sauce. 368
Walnut Pepper Sauce 187
Walnut-Flaxseed Hummus. 212
Wasabi Sauce 192
White Bean Soup 166
Whole Wheat Cauliflower Pizza Dough . . . 349
Whole Wheat Pizza Dough 348
Whole Wheat Vegan Pancakes 127
Zippy Orange Glaze. 194
Zucchini Muffins with Cinnamon-Crumb
Topping. 323

Notes

Notes

Notes